WHEN WILL JESUS BE ENOUGH?

WHEN WILL JESUS BE ENOUGH?

Reclaiming the Power of Worship

Derek Joyce
and Mark Sorensen

Abingdon Press
Nashville

WHEN WILL JESUS BE ENOUGH?
RECLAIMING THE POWER OF WORSHIP

Library of Congress Cataloging-in-Publication Data

Joyce, Derek, 1975–
When will Jesus be enough? : reclaiming the power of worship / Derek Joyce and Mark Sorensen.
    p. cm.
Includes bibliographical references.
ISBN 978-0-687-65231-0 (pbk. : alk. paper)
1. Worship. 2. Public worship. I. Sorensen, Mark. II. Title.

BV10.3.J69 2008
264—dc22

2007031513

08 09 10 11 12 13 14 15 16 17—10 9 8 7 6 5 4 3 2 1
MANUFACTURED IN THE UNITED STATES OF AMERICA

CONTENTS

INTRODUCTION

Don't you just love those moments when you *try* to put a worship service together and all of a sudden, God shows up? I love it when God shows up. *Um, this is not what we had in mind in staff meeting, but, OK, Lord—we will go with You here.*

It was the Thursday before Easter. We were having a somewhat traditional service where there was a lot of reflection and silence as numerous passages were being read, taking us into the story of Jesus before he was led away to be crucified. The space was set up to resemble the Upper Room, and as the crowd gathered, the service began. As we neared the end of the evening, a man dressed as Jesus came from the back of the room. He walked right down the middle of the crowd, slowly, reaching the altar at the front. He turned and faced the people in the room and silently went through the communion rituals. He motioned for us to come and partake in the sacrament. It really was beautiful in all the silence—but silence gives way to noise, and something happened that night that none of us ever saw coming. And it came in the form of a small child.

After our "Jesus" had finished serving communion to those in the room, he smiled and walked down the center of the room to exit the back of the worship space. Then it happened. A small five-year-old girl broke from her mother's grip and made a beeline to Jesus. She threw her arms around him and just embraced him. In the moment of silence, all that could be heard was the little girl's words, "I love you, Jesus. I love you so much."

She got it! She understood that the only thing of any true value was Jesus Christ himself. Everything that occurred that night pointed toward Jesus as the all-satisfying desire of our hearts.[1] Everything that occurs, everything that we participate in should point to Jesus Christ. The question is, *Is this a picture of worship in the church we serve today?*

Allow us to give you a little background about the heart of this book and what you are in store for in the pages to come. Several months back, we were speaking at the Large Church Initiative Conference at a United Methodist church in Washington, D.C., and we were laying out the very things you will find in this book. The class session was titled "There Is No Box." (Coincidentally, at the same time another class was being taught titled "How to Step Outside the Box." Oops!) We found ourselves in a small choir room in the basement of the church and, to be honest, we were not sure what kind of reaction or attendance we would get for the session we were teaching. Ah, but God has a wonderful sense of humor; and at the beginning of our session, we found it packed with senior pastors, associate pastors, youth directors, and others of all ages. It was glorious.

So the session ended, and we opened the floor for a few questions. The first one caught us off guard but was terrific. The question? "Who *are* you guys?" Now this question caused both Derek and me to smile because this was one that we both had spent some time talking about in regards to teaching this session. We asked ourselves, *Do we really spend time listing our credentials, or instead, do we just get into the meat of the study and let the Scriptures and encountering Christ be enough?* We opted for the latter. Now, I am a public speaker and body language says a lot in a question, and I will never forget our new friend's body language. He was arched forward in his chair at about forty-five degrees and he seemed a tad frustrated, as if to imply that he had been waiting for this answer for the past ninety minutes. Also, there were some hidden questions inside this one question that shouted, *What are your credentials? What seminary did you go to? What size church do you work for? How successful are you at doing this?* So let us put you at ease from the start and tell you that we *initially* had absolutely no idea what we were doing.

Mark: I graduated with a degree in communications and a minor in radio and television, and also worked in radio as a disc jockey for nine years. It was at the conclusion of my radio career that God pulled me kicking and screaming into the ministry— The United Methodist Church to be more precise—where I have served for ten years working in youth ministry, college ministry, and leading contemporary worship.

Derek: I graduated from Louisiana Tech University in 1997 with a degree in aviation, which I think adequately qualifies me for ministry. (You can laugh here.) I have worked with college students, young adults, and youth for nine years. Having tasted and seen the goodness of God in my life, I am compelled to work so that others may have the same joy.

Currently we serve at First United Methodist Church in downtown Shreveport, Louisiana. Our church has a membership of four thousand people, and we have an average attendance of twelve hundred on any given Sunday (that is, of course, assuming that the LSU football team does not have a home game scheduled and it is not hunting season). Our church website is www.fumcshreveport.org. While we are throwing out websites, let us give you a few more that concern worship and what we are doing creatively in our church. The first is www.declareloudly.org. This is the website for our Sunday evening worship service called "Declaration," which you will hear more about in the chapters to follow. At that site you will find pictures, scriptures, and detailed information on each of the worship services we have done. Feel free to take the ideas and use them in your own personal study or worship settings. All truth is God's truth. *Claim it!* And if it works, praise God. And if it doesn't? It was "the fault of those Louisiana boys."

Mark: One other site I recommend is my own personal site, www.mark-sorensen.com. I am always writing new music, posting devotions, and updating the lyrics and chords to the worship songs for anyone interested. I also host a MySpace profile that lists my own personal calendar and when and where I am traveling and doing concerts around the country. Find me there at www.myspace.com/marksorensenband.

One of the greatest joys we have experienced is traveling and speaking to people across the country about worship and what it looks like making scripture come to life. We enjoy getting feedback and response to the topics we discuss. Please feel free to fill us in on your experiences and what God is doing in your life and church. Our emails are listed in the back of the book, and we would love to hear from you!

It is our strong conviction that all of life is about the glory of God. We seek to live for the glory of God, reveal the glory of God, so that others may know the glory of God. So for the next few pages come along with us for the journey as we seek to explore encountering Christ not only in thought but also in practice. We are going to look at prayer, praise, study, and communion as avenues to encounter the Lord of all creation in worship.

Hopefully the ideas generated in the following pages will spark
something in you that God will then use to further ministry
wherever you serve. Our prayer is that Jesus Christ will be lifted
up and glorified by what we have done, written, and by what is
now and will be coming from your ministries. Hear these words
as you proceed in this journey:

> *The world and the Church await the achievement of the
> dreams you dare to dream and the miracles your reenergized
> ministry will bring.*[2]

CHAPTER 1

JUST GIVE THEM JESUS!

You know, with a chapter title like "Just Give Them Jesus!" need we say more? I think not.

And this is eternal life, that they may know you, the only true God, and Jesus Christ whom you have sent.
—*John 17:3 NRSV*

And all of life comes down to just one thing.
And that's to know you, Jesus, and make you known.
—*Charlie Hall, "One Thing"*

CHAPTER 2

WORSHIP WORTH GIVING YOUR LIFE FOR

This is what I have found to be true. We are called to live as faithful followers of Jesus Christ. We are to demonstrate our love for God by the way we love others. As we love others, we seek to serve them, not ourselves, and teach them in the best manner we know about the truth of Jesus Christ as revealed in the Bible. Through living our lives faithfully in this manner, we hope, pray, and expect God to make himself known in our lives and in the lives of those we serve in ministry. However, it is not our responsibility to control God or to control how people respond to God. It is our responsibility to cultivate the ground, to water, and to provide the garden space in which growth can truly occur.[1]

THERE ARE NO LIMITS!

I am going to make a bold statement here, so indulge me for a moment. I believe we have forgotten the power of the word *worship.* Worship is something amazing. It is a gift from God to us. Do me a favor. Put the book down for a moment. Find a sheet of paper and write down the word *worship.* What does worship mean to you? How does it make you feel? Come up with your own definition of *worship.* Stop and think for a moment about how beautiful and special worship really is.

We understand that worship is created by God and for God, but we certainly appreciate the overflowing benefits of worship in our lives. Worship gives us the opportunity to connect with—no, that is not quite right—to *know* the Living God of the universe. It means that we know God and God knows us. Let me repeat that last sentence. It

> Worship is this beautiful experience of engaging the Living God.

is much too powerful not to repeat. *We know God and God knows us!* That thought ought to blow your mind wide open at this very moment! We are invited into the presence of God, by God, for the glory of God. This is worship powerfully defined.

It is so unfortunate, then, that worship—this beautiful experience of engaging the Living God—results in a significant deal of frustration. Worship has literally torn some churches apart, creating a "worship war." Maybe here is a good time for a warning. We are in no way seeking to fuel any particular flame regarding worship, save the one that burns for Jesus Christ. This is what we see. People are walking through the doors of our buildings crying out for God. What they need is worship that speaks their language and identifies with their culture, whatever that may be.

Language that identifies with a particular culture can create enormous tension for churches as they seek to preserve their own tradition while desiring to reach out to people who may speak a different language. So let us establish something right at the beginning of this book. We adamantly believe there are multitudes of ways, or languages, in which a person can choose to speak in their worship of Jesus Christ. We do not plan to engage in the war of worship, claiming one way or the other to be *the correct* way to worship. This book is not about style, formulas, or having all the answers. There are many ways to worship. Regardless of the style, location, or time, the important aspect for God is the heart of the worshiper and how we live out our faith— that we worship God in truth as God is revealed in the Bible.

I remember when my son, Nicholas, was ten years old. On a trip, to see family, he was labeled as being "so cute." He looked at me and said, "Dad, I hate that word, *cute*." I asked what he wanted to be called instead of cute, and he looked at me and responded with all the passion a ten-year-old could muster, "Dad, I am beyond description." Let's be honest; people today quite simply do not want to be categorized or labeled. They will rebel, revolt, and run from any notion of categorization. Do not tell them what they like, how they should think, or how they should feel about things. And especially do not tell them how they should worship God. This applies to people of all ages, in all churches.

I have come to understand that most people are hungry for spiritual things. As a result they are coming to our churches expecting to encounter the Living God in fullness and glory. Unfortunately, in many cases they are not finding what the church has promised. Tom Tenny says in his book *God Chasers*, "They looked, or their parents and friends looked and reported, and the spiritual cupboard was bare. There was no presence in the pantry; just empty shelves and offices full of recipes for bread. But the oven was cold and dusty."[2] Tenny says that people come seeking bread, the Bread of Life, only to find, at best in many cases, breadcrumbs, and reminiscing about times when the Bread came down. Upon this discovery that the promise will not be realized, they leave to seek fulfillment and satisfaction in other places. They go to bars, to clubs, to cults, to psychics, to drugs, to pornography, to sexual promiscuity, to Xanga, to MySpace—people will go anywhere in the effort to find acceptance, love, and the promise of something that will deliver them from their pain and confusion. If they do not see the power of God in churches, they will seek the power of another god elsewhere.

> If they do not see the power of God in churches, they will seek the power of another god elsewhere.

One unfortunate story tells of a young woman who used to go to church, and now she hangs out in the local bars. When questioned by a friend about why she would leave the church for a bar, she responded with the simple truth that in six months of being away, only one or two people had inquired about her absence from the church pews. However, when she missed a weekend at the bar, she returned home to find numerous messages on her phone from her "bar friends" wondering if she was OK. This is a person who has found community in a bar rather than in the walls of a church.[3]

People desperately want to encounter the Truth and to see the holy power of the God whom we profess, the only Lord Almighty. They do not want to come to church only to sit quietly and watch passively. They desire to be challenged and engaged. Cameron Strang made this comment, "My generation is discontent with dead religion. . . . We don't want to show up on Sunday, sing two hymns, hear a sermon, and go home. The Bible says we're supposed to die for this thing. If I'm going to do that, this has to be worth something."[4]

People do not want to come to church to be constrained. They desire something more than many of us are currently offering. If this were not a fact, we would not see attendance dropping in our churches today nationwide. Our responsibility as a church is to meet their deepest desires. We are not saying we cater to every whim and fancy, but we are saying it is time we listen to them and learn to speak their languages.

We have incredible news to share. Are you ready? *We do not have to compromise who Jesus is to accomplish this.* We do not even have to sacrifice the traditions of our church. But we must learn to unpackage our worship services in a manner that will reach other, younger generations. We have to learn to be all things to all people in this situation. And we have to do it now.

What if we were to give you a box right now and ask you to fill it with all of the things that come to mind when you think of worship? There is no right or wrong thing here. Just be honest. Be real. Be you. Now don't think about what *you* think *we* think you should be thinking. (Try saying that last sentence three times real fast.) Just think for yourself. OK. Seriously. Here is a box. Now write in it. No one else is looking. Or if you are unsure, get a friend and do this together. Fill in the box with the things of worship.

How did you fare? Were you able to come up with a broad list? If you are like my wife you probably placed them neatly in columns and rows—almost alphabetically. There is nothing wrong with that. That is a style. Or if you are like me, you wrote all over the place, even upside down and maybe struggled to stay inside the lines. There is nothing wrong with that either. That is also a style. Maybe you included some of these things: singing, preaching, praying, and fellowship. Maybe you included the bulletin, the doxology, the Gloria Patri, and the narthex (I still don't know what that is—I just see and hear the word from time to time). Maybe you wrote "healing," "anointing," and "blessing."

Maybe you wrote "scripture," "sixty minutes," "ninety minutes," or "pastor's prayer" (ironically, this can also last for sixty to ninety minutes). Maybe you wrote "traditional," "contemporary," "emerging," "charismatic," "nontraditional," "vespers," or "ancient-future." Maybe this list sparked some things you hadn't thought of. Go back now and write in those ideas. It is OK. Maybe your box looked something like this:

CHOIR

BAND

Hymns *Prayer*

SERMON

CHILDREN'S MESSAGE

CONTEMPORARY

𝕿𝖗𝖆𝖉𝖎𝖙𝖎𝖔𝖓𝖆𝖑

Scripture

Now pay attention to what comes next. This is huge. Are you ready? What if we took away the box? Would that scare you? Would that set you free? What would that mean? Let's see.

BAND CHOIR

Hymns *Prayer*

S E R M O N

CHILDREN'S MESSAGE CONTEMPORARY

𝕿raditional

Scripture

LOOK AT ALL THIS FREE SPACE!!!!

What could you do with all this extra space? The possibilities are endless. Do you remember that moment in your childhood when no one was looking and you took the eight crayons from the box (do you actually remember having a Crayola box with only eight colors?) and just colored *all* over the page? "Look! I am coloring *outside* the lines and I feel great!" Now it is important to note that perhaps the most important thing in this fun little exercise is this truth: when we take away the box, we are not eliminating the contents of the box. There is a very good reason why. Everything that was originally in the box, including what you wrote in your box, is a language of worship. And that language has value. It has value to God, and it has value to the millions of people who speak that same language. Each element satisfies a need, reaches a person, and contributes to the relationship of an individual and a community to their God. They all can work together. We do not believe that we have to eliminate or radically change what occurs in our current worship services. Clearly God is using our churches to reach a significant number of people. If that were not so, we would not see any growth nor would we be hearing testimonies of how God has touched and changed lives throughout existing ministries.

However, for too long we have labeled worship by style. For too long we have sought to market various formulas of worship. It is time to move beyond styles of worship. (Can I get an amen?) It is time to go deeper, to find the truth at the center. The box is what often defines how we order worship. It gives specific contours, offers certain constraints. The point is that sometimes the box becomes only slick packaging that leaves no room for God to act. Worship may be our gift to God; but, in the end, worship belongs to God. We do our congregations and God disservice if we do not intentionally leave room for the Spirit to move.

By taking away the box, we also position ourselves to learn the value of multiple languages of worship. And we can do this without eliminating the beautiful traditions of worship, and more important, without compromising the truth of Jesus Christ. (Refer to chapter 1.) Instead of a box, what if we viewed worship as a broad canopy under which we find all these fascinating means of approaching God? Would some of the tensions subside? Would the traditionalists come to see more value in different kinds of music, musicians, and movement? What if someone resonates with David and dances with wild abandon before the presence of the Lord (2 Samuel 6:14)? Or could the nontraditionalists come to view silence as reverent and powerful, allowing themselves to hear the still, small voice of God (Psalm 46:10)?

Are you still with us? More importantly, are you ready to go deeper?

GOD IS EVERYWHERE

I feel that now is an excellent time to go on record with the following statement: Coffee tastes awful. Seriously. And the coffee *I* get is much too expensive. And it is incredibly hard to order, for, you see, I don't just get a "cup of coffee." I get a skinny, no-whip cup of coffee with mocha and heated to a fine 160 degrees. On one of my recent trips to the coffee shop, I was challenged by the barista behind the counter about why I like my drink of choice, and I had no clear answer. She then recommended a different drink that she felt I might enjoy more. When I asked her how she could be so sure, she simply pointed to her nametag, and she didn't have to say any more. Her name was "Faith."

GOD **IS** EVERYWHERE

Throughout the Bible, people encounter God in a variety of settings. The Bible does not give one end-all format about how God interacts with God's people. God reveals His power by providing a ram caught in a thicket, by leading as a pillar of fire by night and a cloud during the day, by saving in the parting of the waters, by revealing in the bush that was burning yet not consumed, by moving as a mighty rushing wind, and by inspiring as a flame of fire behind closed doors. God inhabits the praises of His people when they sing of God's goodness and meets them in their pain when they are covered by sackcloth and ashes.

THE ONE BIG THING

There really is no restriction on how God's people can worship. There is only one requirement—that they come before the throne of God with honest and sincere hearts. Everything else is miniscule by comparison. Worshiping God is a matter of the heart; and if the heart is not true, then the actions of the people will be detestable unto the Lord (Isaiah 1:10-17; Jeremiah 6:20, 7:21-23; Amos 5:21-24). That is a terrifying statement, but how true! God wants us to love him with our heart, soul, mind, and strength. God asks that we love our neighbor as ourselves. Nothing but our total life is acceptable to God, because God wants us to live and breathe in one accord to bring in God's kingdom.

Empty sacrifice and mere words are always insufficient. Instead God desires that we worship him with our whole lives as well as our lips. Empty rituals fall so short of God's intentions for us. But rituals are easy things to fall into; they can lure us into a false sense of comfort. And that is the point: rituals are things. God is a Person and wants a relationship with us. An encounter with God does not come through a set of acts that we perform, but through the Person of Jesus Christ who enables us to do justice, love kindness, and walk humbly with God (Micah 6:8). This is not to say that there is not some value in ritual. It's just that it is so easy to let correct or comfortable ritual be our sole aim and not the means to be in relationship with God.

Even so, we have to be extremely careful not to fall into the trap of ritual. Gathering on Sundays is great. It is a time for celebration, to worship the Lord our God. But if we do not encounter God, then what really are we doing? I hate to think that there could possibly be thousands, if not millions, of people who are simply going through a ritual in their worship service and leave without having encountered God on any level. I know that people are responsible for their own actions and attitudes regarding worship, but we as the church have a responsibility in this as well. I feel a deep and abiding pain for the churches that seemingly go about their rituals with little or no passion. Let me share an example.

It is amazing that three little words like "He is risen" can hold such power, such excitement, and if you have ever had the opportunity to stand before a church congregation on Easter Sunday morning and share them, you know what I am talking about! And what follows is even better; "He is risen, *indeed*." Now, you must know that I have worked for several different senior pastors. It has always been their responsibility to share those words with their congregation until this past Easter Sunday morning. As I looked at the bulletin for my part in the early traditional service,

I saw that I got the opportunity to share that, indeed, Christ was risen. Me! As I approached the pulpit I couldn't keep my joy contained. I walked to the lectern (did I really just write that word?) and boomed the words "He is risen" into the microphone. What followed was a resounding "He is risen, indeed." After I sat back down, the associate pastor leaned over to me, grabbed my arm in a loving way and said, "Well, if they weren't awake, they certainly are now."

How beautiful a tradition this is! Later that same Sunday as I began to lead worship in the contemporary service, I started worship with the same Easter morning anticipation and looked the crowd in the eyes and declared, "Christ is Risen!" What followed, I hadn't anticipated—crickets. The sound of doughnuts being munched on and coffee being slurped. *No one replied with anything!* One guy, literally with a doughnut in his hand, just sort of shrugged to imply, "If you say so." (Gulp.) Here is an example of a contemporary crowd that missed the richness and beauty of tradition!

My heart goes out in grief for people who have grown up in churches, yet tell me they don't know God. I know people who can give you the complete history of their church. They can retrace the steps of John Wesley, John Calvin, or whoever, depending on the tradition, sing the ancient hymns from memory, and tell you the names of every usher from the day the church doors opened, but they remain confused about who Jesus Christ is. Oh, I can only imagine how this breaks the heart of God. Yes, God is looking for so much more than just empty rituals and long, distinguished church stories. God desires, and the world needs, people who will live with passion and wild abandon for the name and ministry of Jesus Christ.

I absolutely love this statement, "Catch on fire with enthusiasm and people will come for miles to watch you burn." [5] That is such a powerful image. Could it actually be that Jesus was serious when he made the statement, "You are the light of the world. A city built on a hill cannot be hid" (Matthew 5:14 NRSV)?

Let's ask ourselves an honest question. Is your church burning ablaze with the fire of Jesus Christ? Are we ignited by the Holy Spirit in all that we do, or are we more or less going through the motions of ritualistic worship? Are we truly seeking to glorify Jesus? Are we doing everything we can, pouring all our resources out in an effort to reach people for the cause of Christ? Are we teaching our existing congregations to worship the Lord their God with the whole of their being, inside and outside the walls of churches and homes?

This is the goal of this book—that you dedicate yourself to declaring the truth of Jesus Christ with your life—loudly. Our hope is that by loudly declaring the truth of Jesus with your life, you will reclaim the power of worship for the church.

When we plan worship, we do so through a service that allows expression as God so leads. If we want people to live in faith outside restrictive boxes and feel free to follow where God leads, our worship has to help prepare them for that kind of living. We want to cultivate a worship environment where people will feel comfortable worshiping God through confessing, singing, shouting, standing in honor, kneeling, dancing, making a joyful noise, testifying, playing musical instruments, raising hands, or sitting in silence. Rick Warren states, "Where you worship is not as important as *why* you worship and *how much* of yourself you offer to God when you worship."[6] Worship in its truest sense is our giving ourselves freely and fully to God, no strings attached.

Worship is our response to God's grace given to us, unmerited and unearned.

So in all of this, what we are really communicating is that we cannot lead a service for any congregation by just picking a worship style. We cannot sell people on a style or a ritual or a tradition. That will simply not do. It is not enough. Slavishly adhering to style, ritual, or tradition for its own sake, will create a generation or generations of people who may know a lot about the church and its history. They may know a lot about God, but tragically they may not *know* God.

First John 1:1-4 establishes a beautiful and powerful way to lead. It states:

> We write you now about what has always existed, which we have heard, we have seen with our own eyes, we have looked at, and we have touched with our hands. We write to you about the Word that gives life. He who gives life was shown to us. We saw him and can give proof about it. And now we announce to you that he has life that continues forever. He was with God the Father and was shown to us. We announce to you what we have seen and heard, because we want you also to have fellowship with us. Our fellowship is with God the Father and with his Son, Jesus Christ. We write this to you so we may be full of joy.

This passage is absolutely full of sensory elements; it is almost overwhelming. It begins with the truth of Jesus Christ. He is the *Word*, eternally existing with the Father. He is *Truth*. This truth made known to us. And here is the beautiful part about all of this, what John wrote then, we still claim today! We hear, see, touch—in short, we know God in the person of Jesus Christ. This is not some abstract theory. This promise holds just as true to our generation today as it did then. Praise God!

Is there any better place to start? It is one thing to spout off facts about something you think is interesting. It is a completely other thing to speak or share about something that you know because you have heard, seen, and touched it firsthand. I heard this thought explained once like this: you can be a scientist and work for NASA for fifty years. You can hold a doctorate and recite every scientific fact about the stars, cosmos, and the Milky Way. *That* is knowledge. But an amazed eight-year-old lying on his back staring up into the heavens on one of those nights that every star is available for preview—that is an encounter. "Knowledge of" is not the same as "encounter with." People in your congregation want encounters.

It is well known that today's people want to have an "experience." But they want more than a transient high; they want to experience authentic relationship—the kind that they can only have with God. That kind of relationship, one based on an encounter bigger than you, has power. It is inspired with passion because a life has been filled with the Holy Spirit about the truth of God. It makes Psalm 34:8 come alive, "Taste and see that the LORD is good" (NIV). When we can share about the goodness of God because we have tasted, touched, and seen it ourselves, people are going to listen. So the question that naturally follows for me regarding our churches is this, *Are we allowing people to taste, to hear, to see, and to touch or feel the Giver of all life? Are we engaging people? Are they being challenged to engage God?*

I love the end of the 1 John passage. John talks about fellowship. Fellowship is found first in God. From the overflow of the joy of that fellowship, we seek to invite others into it. This is why we share. This is why we lead. This is why we do all of the things that we do in an effort to reach people—because we want their joy to be complete in Christ. Only in Christ will we or anyone else know the fullness of joy that is intended for us by God. This is good news! Who doesn't want joy? This is where we begin and where we seek to end—knowing the One who has always existed from the beginning. Just give them Jesus.

When we know God and know that we are loved by God, we can then move into powerful and passion-filled ministry. We begin to notice that God is at work all over the place. He is at work in our lives, in the lives of our friends and families, and even in the lives of some of the most disgusting people you can imagine. Yes, that person! There is no limit to how God moves. There is no boundary, no box, for the Holy Spirit. We cannot contain God and we should not try. We should only seek to work with him, noticing where God is moving and join with him there.[7]

This is not original. You have heard this before, but many of your people are not living it. The Apostle Paul was brilliant. We read in the Acts of the Apostles that Paul went to Athens on one of his journeys and found God already at work there. The people were worshiping a ridiculous number of gods. They wanted to make sure they had all their bases covered. You never know which god you will need at any given time. And just to be sure, they even had an altar to a god they didn't even know, but maybe thought they might need to know. This story is tragic, fascinating, and humorous all at the same time. Can you imagine the chaos in the lives of these people? Everyone is running around trying to give their time and energy to all these gods that ultimately prove powerless and meaningless. Thank goodness we are a different people today. Or are we?

So Paul walks into this environment, sees the inscription, "TO A GOD WHO IS NOT YET KNOWN." Beautiful. God is at work. God has been prepping these people for some time. And Paul sees it. He sees it because he knows God. He knows that God cannot be contained, that God is always at work. Paul has eyes to see and ears to hear. He knows the truth about this God and he shares it with the people. He finds truth and he claims it! How simple is that?! But there was no church founded in Athens by Paul. God used him for more prep work.

An old college buddy and I used to go out and party on a regular basis. We were always together. We played soccer together and drank together. It was a great friendship. Then the Lord grabbed hold of me. I had to sever that relationship for a time because I knew that I wasn't strong enough, wasn't mature enough, to be around my friend. Because we played a sport together, it was only a matter of time before we started talking again. The Lord provided the strength for me, and I began to really show the change that had occurred in my life. We continued to be friends for some ten years. During that time we spoke regularly. He would share with me his wild stories. I would sit and listen, laughing at some, reminiscing about others, and occasionally trying to speak gentle truth to him about his life. Ten years. One morning he called me. He confessed to me about the night before. I could tell there was something deeper going on. He told me how he woke up in the middle of the night and started watching the movie *Constantine*.

Now I have to stop here and ask if you have ever seen this movie. I have. I am generally a Keanu Reeves fan (one of the few, I guess). But this movie was completely laughable. It was full of the worst Christian clichés, the most absurd perspective on angels and demons—and I can be generous in appreciation for artistic license in movies. I didn't know whether to laugh or cry.

Back to my friend. He tells me about a scene where the angel Gabriel was talking about how stupid humans are—about how all we have to do is accept the love of God, namely *His* grace, and yet we refuse to do so. In this moment my friend got it. He awakened to the reality of Jesus Christ. We wept and laughed together. It was beautiful!

Now, I could argue with how anyone could experience the reality of Christ through this movie; or I could accept that God was at work in my friend's life, awakening his heart in a seemingly unorthodox situation. I choose to embrace that God is always at work. I see that truth and I am claiming it. Beautiful.

God is everywhere.

CHAPTER 3

RECLAIMING THE POWER OF WORSHIP THROUGH PRAISE

Shout for joy to the LORD, all the earth.
  Worship the LORD with gladness;
  come before him with joyful songs.
Know that the LORD is God.

  It is he who made us, and we are his;
  we are his people, the sheep of his pasture.
Enter his gates with thanksgiving
  and his courts with praise;
  give thanks to him and praise his name.

For the LORD is good and his love endures forever;
  his faithfulness continues through all generations.
  —Psalm 100 NIV

ROBUST PRAISE AND WORSHIP

I t was one of the first times I had gone to summer camp as a
youth director. I will never forget how hot it was in east Texas
that summer, nor will I forget how much I just don't like eating camp food. There is something about the words "fried" and
"mystery meat on a stick" that just don't mix with me; call me
picky. It was the first full day of camp, and we were in morning
chapel. We were given instructions to take some Bible verses we
were given and that evening come into worship and do a skit or
in some way act out what the verses meant to us. I remember how
excited my small group was to do that! We were doing John 3:16
all day long. We brainstormed and came up with this beautiful
parable to the scripture we were going to do for the entire camp
that night.

It was 9:00 p.m. and we gathered in the chapel for the start of
the worship service. (Did I mention that was two hours past my
bedtime? The sacrifices I make for the Lord!) All of the youth were
gathered, and there must have been 200 of us crammed into this
tiny chapel. My heart was pumping from the excitement of seeing
the Scriptures, God's incarnate word, *come to life* in the moments
that followed. The candles were lit on the altar; the evening light
was coming through the stained glass windows and everything was
so beautiful that the Holy Spirit took over in me, and I let out a
"Woo hoo" in excitement. Have you ever been there? Oh, how I
pray you have! It was a sound of joy, anticipation, sheer, unbridled
"I can't *wait* to see what God is going to do in this place and
through these young people!" That is when I felt "the hand."

She was an older lady, small in stature but, *man*, did she ever
have a grip on her. She must have been a schoolteacher (I say

24

that for the sake of my wife, the ultimate schoolteacher with a grip) who also came to camp that year as a counselor. She grabbed that muscle on the side of my neck that sort of incapacitates you, while, at the same time, sends a sharp pain to the brain that says, "Warning, this hurts." And in response to my "woo who," to the anticipation of what God was going to do, she responded with a very loud, "Shhhh. . . . *Worship* is about to begin." In other words, she was saying to me, "Be *quiet.* Church is not the place for your *noise.*" I mean no disrespect in the following seven words, but I must be honest—I just can't conform to that thought.

This is a highlighted, bold, underlined statement, so choose your color, whether pink or yellow—**Satan seeks to silence the praise of God's children**. I believe that with all of my heart. Think about it. Have you ever just had this encounter with God and your heart couldn't contain your passion? But no sooner than you are filled with that joy, the world begins to immediately suck it out of you. Should we be surprised? I believe Peter when he says, "Your enemy the devil prowls around like a roaring lion looking for someone to devour" (1 Peter 5:8 NIV). That's ME! That's YOU! And get ready, church, because Satan seeks to *devour* your praise.

If you are ever having a bad day, take a look at the life of Paul in the New Testament. Talk about persecution around every corner. One story in particular can be found in the book of Acts. Paul and Silas are on their way to the place of prayer when a fortune-teller with an "evil spirit" follows closely behind them, mocking them by saying, "These men are servants of the Most High God, who are telling you the way to be saved" (Acts 16:17 NIV). (*I love that comment.* In a day that most of the religious leaders didn't understand the message of Jesus Christ, the demons certainly understood who Jesus was.) After taking this for several days, Paul and Silas had had enough and they cast the evil spirit out of her. This, however, did not sit well with the men who made a profit from the woman who was able to make money for them through her fortune telling. So the scripture reads that Paul and Silas were taken before the officials and an uproar quickly rose up against them (refer back to the previous comment, "the devil prowls . . . looking . . . to devour"). They were ordered to be "stripped" and "beaten"; and the Bible says that after they had been "severely flogged," they were shackled and thrown into prison.

Now do me a favor. Put yourself in that place and time. Would the very thought of praise come to mind? I am not convinced that that would be in my vocabulary. I am a terrific whiner. However, this was not in the heart of Paul and Silas. Take a look at the following verse taken from *The Message* Bible, Acts 16:25: "Along about midnight, Paul and Silas were at prayer and singing a robust hymn to God. The other prisoners couldn't believe their ears."

"Robust." Now there is a word in the English language that we need to use more. Here are two guys, beaten and bleeding, and they choose to enter into the throne room of God's mercy with a "robust hymn to God." And what follows that robust praise? The other prisoners could not believe their ears. Beautiful. We give our praise, *not* because of our circumstances, not for any person on *this* earth, but to the one *worthy* of our praise! And it was through that act of praise on that very evening, that a jailer's life and his family's life were forever changed. All because of robust worship and praise before the Lord.

VERTICAL PRAISE AND WORSHIP

I was leading worship on a Sunday morning at a church I was serving in East Texas where I heard the pastor share a beautiful message about how our worship should not be horizontal, but instead it should be vertical. It should go beyond the human-made structure of the church building and then rise and fall at the feet of the one *worthy* of our praise. I remember sitting there thinking, "Yes, Lord, here is someone who *gets* what our praise is about!" And what beautiful teaching it was. Isn't that really a message we all need to hear? I left with such inspiration and, coincidentally, closed the service with a song that said, "Let everything that has breath, praise the Lord."

That following Monday morning, it was time for our staff meeting. I sat in the meeting and was still empowered by the words of the message from the previous day. And imagine my shock when the senior pastor who had just preached the "vertical vs. horizontal" message looked at me and said, "By the way, I would appreciate it if you would pick some songs that *everyone* in the congregation knows. My wife sat in the service and didn't know a single one of your *worship songs* that you led." My jaw dropped. (*But what about vertical worship?*) It became very real to me in that moment that he had given a message but missed its deepest meaning.

It absolutely breaks my heart to think that beautiful acts of praise are dividing some churches straight down the middle. And let me tell you, the battle is real and happening all across the world on a daily basis. One of my favorite stories is of the little traditional church I worked for where, on a whim, we grabbed a tambourine and played it on a song we were doing for special music. I know, what was I thinking, huh? Immediately after the service, I went to go get it and I noticed that it was gone. It totally was not where I had put it; and, after only a short period of time, I realized what had happened—someone took it. As I began inquiring what had happened to it, I was told by an unnamed source that it would *never* be seen in the sanctuary again; (gulp). (I just know in my heart of hearts that that little fish-shaped tambourine was dipped in cement and dropped off into the Red River. Alas, I will never know.)

On the other side of the spectrum, I have played for contemporary services where there was such a feeling of "us versus them" that praise members boycotted the sanctuary because that was not where contemporary worship was "meant to be." I feel quite certain that if I opened the floor right now to you, you could give more of the same stories. Again, let me ask you. *Is this really what God had in mind when it comes to our praise?* I just don't think so.

Our planning team at First Church gathered one evening and we decided to tackle a worship service that answered this question: "What would an evening of praise look like if we *only* focused on praise and nothing else?" We went further. We thought, "How great would it be if our praise went beyond the walls of the church and into the greater community that God has placed our church in?" It is actually quite an exciting thought, isn't it? Imagine praise *so loud* that it goes beyond the walls of the church and spills out to the greater community. So, we took our service to the roof.

Now, off the bat, let me alleviate any concerns you may have. The roof is not sloped, so this was not an unsafe adventure. We happen to have a Sunday school classroom on our third floor that opens up to a fenced-in roof area. We put rugs down and moved our church sound system outside. So for the evening we entertained the neighborhood with the beautiful act of praise under the stars. We sang songs like, "All Creatures of Our God and King" and "Here I Am to Worship." The sunset was beautiful and the music was just loud enough. There were several times when we opened the microphone and invited all to come and share Scriptures of praise or moments of affirmation to God.

Another element of praise that we included that evening was an old upright chalkboard that we borrowed from a classroom in the church. It sat literally in the middle of the worship space with tons of chalk available. As we started the evening, we pointed out the chalkboard that sat before us and just gave the instructions that we can worship God through the act of journaling. We invited those there that night to come and write down their praise on the board. We wanted them to be free to take their time to praise through using chalk however they saw fit. It was beautiful. At the conclusion of the service, there was not an inch of space where words did not cover the board. There were comments ranging from, "Jesus, I love you" to "Because of the praise I feel in my heart, I know I am saved!" It was powerful to just see what God was saying to the people who were there on the roof that night. In all, there were close to 100 people who gathered on the roof that evening for worship. There were youth, college students, moms and dads, pastors from the church; it was a vertical experience that went beyond everyone that was there and glorified God in a powerful way!

And now it's your turn. How can you take the element of praise and incorporate it in vibrant ways into your worship? What would a Sunday look like if you just worshiped with praise—you

What would a Sunday look like if you just worshiped with praise?

worshiped through contemporary music, through traditional hymns, through Scriptures of adoration and the psalms of David? Have a fifth Sunday service of worship and praise.

An example of a Sunday service where praise can be expressed came in the form of a service we led on Sunday, December 31, 2006. This may surprise you but we went a bit overboard on the planning of this worship service. We had just finished a study from the Psalms and spent some time looking at Psalm 78:1-2. David is calling for us to celebrate in these verses, to blow our horns in worship for all that God has done. "Well, if we *have* to, David." The sermon title was "Blow It Out Your Horn" (you just have to *love* sermon titles), and for a New Year's Eve the service was pretty packed. As people arrived into the service they were handed a worship bulletin and a party horn. Yes, I said party horn.

At the beginning of the service, Derek made the announcement that "this morning we are here to celebrate what God is doing and what God has in store for His people." Much to my shock, Derek asked the congregation to blow their horns with the music and "let's worship together." It is not every Sunday you get that feeling of singing "Forever" with blow horns, party favors, and kazoos joining you from the congregation, but it was pretty cool. Then came the sermon. We talked a bit about celebration and the need to celebrate with one another the victories that God had given us. Then we opened the floor to any in the congregation who wanted to share. After they shared, we invited the people to blow their horns and celebrate that victory together. The first lady, off the bat, was a visitor who none of us knew. She shared about her son who was in a car accident and was left with months of recovery and the possibility of never walking again. But she shared that what is impossible to many is never impossible in the hands of our God. She said her son was walking again and she wanted to give God the glory. And what followed her testimony? People applauded, cheered, blew their horns, and we celebrated a victory from the hands of God.

Then there was another. His car had been impounded, his insurance was out of date, and he had been convicted because he had not paid his debts. But through the impounding and several tickets he received, (get this) he *celebrated* God holding him accountable and rejoiced that he was current and driving legally now for the first time in several months. Praise God! After twenty minutes (and what could have gone much longer) we closed with a song called "Praise Him" and ended the service shooting off confetti guns and streamers in the worship center.

Talk about a New Year's Eve service to remember. At the suggestion of many, it looks to become a yearly New Year's Eve worship experience! Or, better yet, maybe you can think of ways to worship *beyond* the walls of the church. Find a park. Have your church members bring lawn chairs and food. Make your praise part of your *outreach* and in doing so, through these acts of praise, be kingdom worshipers!

Let us go back one last time and revisit this thought: **What if, within our church buildings, we were making such a bold attempt at our worship through praise that the message of Jesus Christ couldn't be contained within their walls?** I believe that we must understand that praise is so much more than the latest contemporary song backed by the church worship team and singers. (Hide your tambourines, by the way.) Our praise is intended to be vertical, not horizontal. **Understand that the world does not deserve our praise. Our praise should be reserved for the One who gave each of us breath; it is the cry from our hearts to the One who gives and takes away.**

A fellow worship leader, Darlene Zschech, said, "The essence of worship is when your heart and soul, all that is within you, adores, and connects with the Spirit of God. In fact, regardless of how magnificent the musical moments are, unless your heart is fully engaged in the worship being expressed . . . it is still only music. The pure song of a heart that is yearning for more of God, and less of himself, is the music that holds the key to so many victories . . . and delights the heart of our King."[1]

I love it when I encounter those moments of compulsory praise; that is, praise that demands our dancing before the Lord. Allow me to share one of those moments with you. I write music and, to be honest, I listen to the world around me for the lyrics. I was in a church member's office and we were talking about a difficult situation that was going on at the time. The staff member's mom, who happened to be there, just responded with this comment: "We're just going to dance like David over this situation and trust that God has it all under control." I loved that thought, "Dance like David." So I began to pray and write and out of that was born the song "Dance Like David."

> I want to dance like David; I want to lift my song to You.
> I want to dance like David; I want my praise to raise this roof.
> I want to dance like David; I want to fall on my knees in praise.
> I want to dance like David; I want my joy to fill the place.

I want to dance like David; I want to shout the victory.
I want to dance like David;
and dance before the One who dances over me.
I want to dance like David; I want to spill my words of love.
I want to dance like David; I join the angels from above.

Because all creation sings its song to You,
The rocks, they cry, the stars, they shine.
And who am I to be silent?

I want to sing and I want to dance
and I want to lift my heart to You.
I want to laugh and I want to cry
and I want to lose myself in You.
To be set free to spread my wings
to stand before the King of kings.
To climb this hill and stand up strong
and tell this world to whom I belong.

I want to dance.[2]

That Sunday morning in our contemporary service, God led me to sing that song, which was interesting because I hadn't really even finished it. But, I did not question and sang it for special music. By the second verse, the most unexpected thing happened; people started dancing (by "people," I mean two). Now, you must know that we have a pretty kicking worship service at our church, but spontaneous dancing rarely happens. I loved it. Afterwards, one of the congregant praise dancers approached me and simply responded, "I hope that didn't bother you but, in that moment, it was just *wrong* to stay seated." Amen, brother. Amen!

Let me encourage you; give your people different ways to offer praise in worship. But in doing so, remember to always allow room for God to move in worship. If you are looking for some new praise ideas, please visit our website, www.declareloudly.org and take some time to share with us *your* experiences in worship. We would love to hear your stories.

What do you say? Are you ready to join me in a robust hymn to the one who is worthy of our praise? Haven't we been seated in our lives for *much* too long? Come on, brothers and sisters. *Join me!*

> On your feet now—applaud GOD!
> > Bring a gift of laughter,
> > sing yourselves into his presence.
>
> Know this: GOD is God, and God, GOD.
> > He made us; we didn't make him.
> > We're his people, his well-tended sheep.
>
> Enter with the password: "Thank you!"
> > Make yourselves at home, talking praise.
> > Thank him. Worship him.
>
> For GOD is sheer beauty,
> > all-generous in love,
> > loyal always and ever.
> > > —Psalm 100 *Message*

CHAPTER 4

RECLAIMING THE POWER OF WORSHIP THROUGH PRAYER

Prayer is an art that has to be learned.—Peter Forsyth

Remember how we stated that worship is more like a broad canopy under which there are a million forms, or avenues, to encounter the Lord? Prayer is one of them. So let us ask you this question: *When it comes to teaching your church about prayer, what are you teaching? How do you use prayer in your worship?*

At a recent conference we spoke with pastors and laity on just this topic when we asked the question, "How are you teaching your congregations to pray?" After an uncomfortable pause, we found that there was really no good answer to this question. The comment was, "Well . . . we just *pray*." But I would challenge that that isn't *enough*. When it comes to your church *teaching about prayer* verses the church *teaching the congregation to pray*, there is a subtle yet powerful distinction. But if we are not careful, we won't even notice. And that can mean the difference between a people caught on fire with the passion and power of God or people who mainly try to stay awake through the service.

TEACHING ABOUT PRAYER IS CRUCIAL

Obviously, it is essential to have a good, solid theological basis for prayer. After all, if you don't know who you are praying to or what you are praying for, then who knows what, if any, results will come? And even if the results do come, what do they mean? How would you think about them? They could be viewed simply as coincidence, happenstance, or just plain luck. And if there are no tangible or immediate results, then you run the risk of people thinking that it simply proves the point that prayer is stupid and ineffective. For all of these reasons and more, yes, it is absolutely necessary to teach about prayer.

First Thessalonians 5:16-18 states, "Always be joyful. Pray continually, and give thanks whatever happens. That is what God wants for you in Christ Jesus." Some translations conclude with "this is the will of God for you in Christ Jesus." I find it interesting that centered between joy and thanksgiving is prayer. It makes perfect sense to me. In order to have joy and to be able to give thanks, one must cultivate a life of prayer. **Joy and**

> Joy and giving thanks are the natural outpouring of praying continuously.

**giving thanks are the natural outpouring of praying continu-
ously.** But it would be a mistake to stop at that insight, for the
rest is far more compelling. The author states clearly that this—
namely, having joy that results from a lifestyle of prayer and
enables one to give thanks whatever happens—is the will of God
for our lives. Now I don't know about you, but I am always
intrigued when someone lets me in on what God's will is. Who
would have thought it—the will of God is for us to pray, that our
lives might be full of joy, and in everything we might be able to
give thanks because we know from Whom we receive true life.

If you spend any amount of time in the Gospels, you will notice
an event that takes place over and over again. Jesus is constantly
sneaking away to spend some time with his Father. How terrific
is that? You can see Peter and the other disciples telling the
crowds, "Yeah, I'll ask Jesus. Hey, Jesus! . . . Wait, he was *just
here*!?" Check this out—seeking solitude and spending time with
his Heavenly Dad was necessary for *his* ministry. The greater
thought is, *Why should it be any different for our ministry?*

Have a look at the eleventh chapter of the Gospel of Mark,
beginning in verse 15. The passage is particularly intriguing to
me. Jesus goes into the temple fairly disturbed by what the people have made of it. He gets a little holy anger going and before
you know it, he is overturning tables with *much* vim and vigor. I
have always liked this image of Jesus. Not because I enjoy anger,
but because he seems so real to me in this moment.

I also can't help but think of how silly many of our existing
portraits of Jesus are when I read this text. So many pictures por-
tray Jesus as a fragile, delicate figure who might be in danger of
being blown over by a gentle breeze *and* with a lamb around his
neck! The Bible says that Jesus was a carpenter for most of his

life. He didn't begin ministry until about age thirty. So a conservative estimate would give him fifteen to twenty years of working with wood: fashioning, hammering, sculpting, pushing, and pulling. This was no easy job!

I have a carpenter friend who accidentally just put a nail through his hand while framing a home. After emergency surgery and only a couple days' rest, he returned to the job he started. This is one tough man—nothing fragile here. And this is exactly how I see Jesus. He was a carpenter. I presume he had some meat on his bones, and I imagine he could be pretty intimidating if he got a little upset about something. So when he goes and starts flipping tables, I think there is some authority to him. He is upset. He has the attention of the people. And what does he tell them? "My Temple will be called a house for prayer for people from all nations" (Mark 11:17). Wow! Prayer. He quotes the prophet Isaiah here and the point is not easily missed. We are commanded by God to make God's house a house of prayer. If it is anything other than that, it is not fulfilling its established— ordained—purpose. That should make you stop and think. God takes this prayer thing kind of seriously.

Consider also the often quoted passage of 2 Chronicles 7:14. It is a classic *if/then* statement— one of many *bilateral contracts* (God does something and we do something—a shared responsibility) that we discover in the Bible. What we see is that yes, grace and mercy flow freely from God, but we do have some responsibility in our walk with the Lord. "*If* my people (that is, you and me) humble themselves, pray, seek my face, repent (turn from wicked ways), *then* I (God) will hear, forgive, heal."

God's hearing, forgiving, and healing is contingent upon our prayer, which includes humility, seeking God's face, and repentance. When we are faithful to prayer, God is faithful to respond. Now, most people stop here. But I find the next several verses incredibly stimulating in light of Jesus Christ, particularly the resurrection. Verses 15-16 talk about Solomon's temple. This temple was constructed as a place where God would dwell. God declares that He has chosen this temple and He will make it holy and be worshiped there forever. He declares that He will always watch over it and love it.

Let us move to the New Testament. In John 2:19, Jesus says that if people destroy the temple he will restore it in three days. Everyone thinks he is crazy. They quickly remind him it took forty years to build the temple. But Jesus says he is talking about his body. This is key because Jesus has made the declaration that God does not dwell any longer in a physical structure made by humans. When Jesus dies, is buried, rises from the dead, and ascends into heaven, he then pours out his Spirit (the Spirit of God) upon his people. Now we see that the Spirit of God dwells in us. We are the temple.

Continuing on in 1 Corinthians 3:16, we see this thought clarified even more by Paul. We (me, you, our youth groups, our congregations, our college students, the people whom we call the body of Christ)—we are God's temple, and God's Spirit lives in us. We are the place where God dwells! We are to be a *house of prayer*! This gives us a solid biblical foundation for the priority of prayer in our lives. We need to make every attempt to be the house of prayer that God will dwell in and move freely in, that His name will be glorified among all people.

There are good reasons, and no shortage of places, to find the necessity of teaching prayer from a theological standpoint. But let us focus on how are we teaching people to pray and what part prayer plays during worship. I am afraid, for many, prayer is simply something the paid staff participates in—clergy are trained for that kind of stuff—you know, talking to God and such. How many churches have, at best, a one-to two-minute pastoral prayer during worship? But for many thousands of people, worship is the only time they come close to praying. If that is the case, how will they ever grow in their faith? I am reminded of the passage that asks how people will be saved if they never hear the good news. And how will people hear the good news if they are not told? And how will they be told if others are not sent (Romans 10:13-15)?

> ## How are we teaching people to pray in worship?

What if we replace saving with praying? How will people connect with God if they don't know how to pray? And how will people learn to pray if they are not shown or taught? So let me restate the question one last time, *How are we teaching people to pray in worship?*

We may not have all the answers, nor are we claiming to know the best way to pray, nor are we advocating one way of prayer over another. We are simply asking the hard questions and hopefully leading in a manner that is both godly and challenging. We have tried a few things, and some have yielded more positive responses than others. But we all must continue trying and teaching that others may have the opportunity to encounter the Living God.

WORSHIP PLANNING

Let's say we are planning a Wednesday evening worship service, and on the first night, we want to start with the topic

"Prayer." So we ask ourselves, "OK, what if we spent an entire evening focusing on *just* prayer, and rather than us teach that, what if, instead, we *engaged* in it for the evening?" Remember, we view prayer as an avenue of worship. It is a means to worship God. The end result is always encountering God. If it is anything less, if it seeks to glorify itself, or us, then that is a tragedy. So we begin with the most basic form of prayer that we can and we build on that.

A.C.T.S.

Have you ever heard of the acronym "A.C.T.S."? It stands for *Adoration, Confession, Thanksgiving,* and *Supplication.* Here is what we did. We took the gym area of our church and completely transformed it into four stations of prayer. You guessed it! One station for each: one for adoration; one for confession; one for thanksgiving; and one for supplication. But that wasn't all. We outlined a *huge* cross with candles so that each station was placed at the end of a cross arm. (Oh, how our beloved trustees just *love* it when we use fire in the church. Come to think of it, that would stem from a previous Wednesday night encounter when one of our banners caught fire in worship. More on that story later.)

Adoration was at the head. Supplication was at the right. Thanksgiving was at the left. And confession was at the foot of the cross. It made sense to us to put confession at the foot. Most people like to kneel before the Lord to confess (assuming they like to confess in the first place). So there we were, with an altar for each station of prayer. As the people gathered, we asked them to gather in the large central portion of the cross on the floor. We gave them each a notebook and a pencil. We told them that we were going to be spending the night in prayer—not talking about it—actually praying. We explained the stations and invited them to spend just ten minutes at each station. They could pray however they chose, whether that was journaling, praying out loud, or reflecting silently. At each station there was a person who was available to lead them. That person's role was to simply define the type of prayer (adoration, and so on), give biblical precedent for it (read a scripture relating to it), and give a short example. This was to last no longer than two minutes and then everyone was turned loose to pray. And at the conclusion of each session, we led the doxology with a guitar and some percussion, and that was the signal to go to the next station.

Adoration

Mark: Let us think about adoration. Can you think of a time when you were left speechless before God? For example, I was on a mission trip with a group of youth in Mexico, and each evening we spent group time outside, debriefing on the day's events. I will never forget the nights. The place that we stayed was outside of the city and, on any one of the nights we spent outside, I was left completely in awe at the *amazing* expanse of stars that were available for our viewing. Growing up in the city totally blinds you to the fact that the heavens are an *amazing* creation!

Derek: I remember when I was in college. We were on a retreat in the mountains of Arkansas. The beauty of college retreats is that there are seldom 10:00 p.m. bedtimes. On one particular night, we walked down to the lake and lay there on the dock staring up at the skies. It was a clear night—so clear that you could see the haze of the Milky Way. We lay there in silence for what had to be an hour. Finally, someone said, "What is man that You, oh God, are mindful of us?" It was a quote from Psalm 8, and it reminded us of the greatness of God. We continued to adore God well into the morning. It is still one of the most powerful memories I have of being in the presence of God. So to create an adoration station, we attempted to bring those images into our church gymnasium. To help accomplish this we had images of the glory of God's creation being shown on screens. A simple Google search for galaxy images returned 702,000 pictures. This should be enough pictures to get you started. Looking at these images, you quickly become lost in the beauty and majesty of the Lord and find yourself in a place of adoration.[1]

I remember very clearly on that evening seeing people just lost in wonder at the images that ran before their eyes. Some journaled, but most saw, and just for a few moments amidst the busyness of their lives, they slowed down enough to get lost in the adoration of an amazing God.

Thanksgiving

Thanksgiving is giving thanks for all that God has done. For this station, we had pieces of paper and pens available and encouraged people to spend time reflecting on *what* we have to give thanks about. We sometimes sing these words in church: "You give and You take away, but my heart will choose to say, / Lord, blessed be Your name."[2]

I often wonder if we realize what is coming out of our mouths and hearts. For a few moments in the silence that evening we wrote down ALL things, the good and the bad, and just spent time giving THANKS for all that is given to us. Ironically our station leader later told us that she was at such a place in her life that she was challenged to lead others into giving thanks. But that is the true reality of living. Giving thanks means recognizing that every good and perfect gift comes from above and that God is always near. It can also mean a time of sorting through tragedies we all experience in our lives and realizing that what others intend as evil, God may use for good.

Supplication

Supplication is a fancy word for praying for other people, asking God to move in their lives. Or to quote the great philosopher Mr. Webster, it is "to ask humbly and earnestly of." It is believing that God will meet a need, physically, financially, emotionally, relationally, and spiritually. It is believing God will intervene in a life to cause someone to stop, recognize the glory and the power of the Lord Almighty, and seek to know God and make Him known. It is begging for people to come to a knowing and saving relationship with Jesus Christ. It is praying and believing that loved ones will be delivered from the bondage of sin in all of its malicious forms. It is coming against Satan and his minions in the mighty and powerful name of Jesus Christ, that chains will be broken and lives will be set free for the glory of the Living Lord. It expects a mighty release of the Holy Spirit into the most desperate of situations resulting in faith, hope, and love in lives, churches, and communities. To this end we set up a globe to see the broad picture. We also tore out pages of our phone book to give people specific names to lift before the Lord.

Confession

Confession became something we did not completely expect, although we secretly hoped for. We set up an entire booth. It was sectioned off with curtains. On the inside there was an altar, a kneeling rail, incense to burn and candles to light. You literally had to pull the curtain back to enter. Our leader for this station just knelt at the altar and spent the evening weeping through various prayers of confession. This totally blew us away. We gave him no script. We just told him to lead as God led him, being sensitive to the Holy Spirit. He would later tell us (and to be honest, I believe he actually apologized for this) that he could not help weeping because he sensed the heart of God for the people coming in. Wow!

It is important to note here another thing. We (Mark and Derek) did not lead any of these stations. **WARNING: REVOLUTIONARY CONCEPT ALERT** Here is what we did: We sought out laypeople with a heart for prayer and asked them to be part of the evening. *I have great news, brothers and sisters*—we don't have to do *everything*! There are people in our congregations and ministries who are not ordained, do not have any desire to go to seminary or serve as a pastor of a church, but have a serious desire to serve Christ and lead others in that endeavor. All we have to do is ask. And honestly, if we build the church around God's ministry, isn't this what Christ is calling us to do in the first place?

It was a wonderful sight to see everyone participating in the service. People actually prayed for forty to fifty minutes. They did it. Not the clergy. Not the leadership. The people. You could hear the scribbles of pencils on the paper. You could hear people weeping, both sorrowfully and joyfully. You could see smiles on faces. You could feel the presence of God. After that night we had several people come and tell us how much they enjoyed it. One person actually said, "I wish I could pray like that all the time." Another said, "I have never prayed for that long in my entire life.

It was amazing. I felt closer to God than I have ever felt." I remember leaving that experience that night, not thinking, "Man, I pulled off another great program," but in total awe that, that night, God showed up and moved in such a powerful way. Hey, church—that exactly is why we need to teach people how to pray and give them opportunities to practice prayer.

COMING TO A SUNDAY MORNING SERVICE NEAR *YOU*!

Now here is another thought. What would your Sunday morning worship service look like if you did this very same thing? What if you took a month and you did a series on prayer? Now we are not talking about four 30-minute, 5-point with 3 subpoints each, Bible-shaking, "you sit and listen" sermons. Nobody wants to hear that and many don't like to do it either. But that is exactly our point. Lead prayer not by teaching about prayer but by engaging in prayer with your congregation. This is an exciting thought!

It is a special person who can take the topic of adoration and make that boring. Consider this: You could take your sanctuary, and for one Sunday take each corner of the room and just encourage people to spend time in prayer. Let your laypeople or staff use some serious creativity to lead people through adoration, confession, thanksgiving, and supplication. Maybe it is a special Wednesday evening prayer service in your gymnasium. Maybe it is a fall outside event and you are just calling for an evening of prayer. Pastors, maybe you prepare your congregation for the idea that you are taking the following Sunday off and, instead, calling them to join you in prayer for the morning. I know. There are things that have to happen like offering and children's time, but, again, we ask you to consider, would it be so wrong to just challenge the order of the Sunday morning bulletin? Sometimes rocking the boat is a good thing. If Jesus can sleep through a rocking boat, maybe, just maybe, we will survive and not perish.

PRAYER WALK

During another worship service, we met, gathered in our normal spot, went over a few housekeeping things, and then again asked the group to trust us. (I am finding that this question now strikes a small sliver of fear in their hearts.) When the question arose as to where we were going and what we were doing, we told them we were going to Jericho. We journeyed outside to a small courtyard and garden area on the side of our church. We sat down, sang a few songs without musical accompaniment (it is possible), and then prepared for the night. We set up what we were doing by looking at the passage in Joshua about taking the city of Jericho (chapter 6). This is such a familiar passage for many of our people that we needed to look at it again from a different perspective—one of entering into the story. How real the word of God becomes when we place ourselves inside the story.

We began with this brief background. The people of God, the Hebrews, have been wandering around in the desert for some forty years. An entire generation has died and they are awaiting entrance into the land promised them by God. Their leader, Moses, has recently died as well, and Joshua has been appointed in his place. Joshua hears these great and encouraging words from the Lord, "Be strong and brave . . . be strong and brave . . . I commanded you to be strong and brave. Don't be afraid, because the LORD your God will be with you everywhere you go" (Joshua 1:6-9). And where they are going is to the land that they were promised from so long ago. The original promise for Abram was that the nations would be blessed in order to be a blessing. It seems to me that God desired, at least in part, for His people to inhabit the land in order that they may grow in their knowledge and understanding of what it means to be the people of God, but also that they may bless the other nations around them.

Jericho was the first phase of their conquest—more than just a militaristic aspiration. I will be the first to admit that I have a seriously hard time with the fact that they *devote* the city and everything in it to God. After marching around the city, they devote it by killing all within the city walls. But I hold to the truth that God desired to bless His people for the sake of others. In God's good and perfect will, the walls had to come down. What if, in our churches today, we sought to have walls come crashing down in order that people might come to know and fear the Lord? What if the walls that came down were not primarily physical, but they were relational, spiritual, economical, racial, and more? What if the people in our communities saw that we cared for them, not only for our buildings and public reputation? What if the walls came down?

So we challenged the congregation to march around our church, about four city blocks. We challenged folks to seriously pray for the community around us, for the staff and members of the church, and pretty much for anyone that we saw as we were walking. And so we walked. And we prayed. We all went together and for the first time in a long time, we recognized that we were not alone in our community. There were drug houses just a few blocks away, so we prayed for them. There were homeless people living in abandoned homes and buildings right beside our church, and so we prayed for them. We turned the corner, and began walking toward the city and the contrast was stark. Behind us was poverty. In front of us was the business community. And so we prayed for the business leaders, and the police officers, and the judges, and the councilmen and -women. For me, personally, one of the greatest moments came in the form of a man who appeared homeless who met us on the last leg of the journey.

The day before we held this prayer walk, I was very bold in my prayer and asked God to show up on the walk; through a person, through a situation, somehow. Just "make Yourself known to us." As we approached the last corner of the last block, there was a man crossing the road in front of us. I remember my thought was, *Could this be the one that God has placed in our path?* Like many who wander in the neighborhood around our facility, he was dirty and looked to have not bathed in a while. He watched us as we got closer to him, and then it happened. He stopped from his traveling and, slowly, took off his baseball cap and, with such reverence and peace, bowed his head and said not a word but joined us in the encounter in prayer as we walked by. It is true. Nearly everyone saw the man, and was amazed that without saying a word, this man was able to recognize something holy about what we were doing.

At one point in the walk one of our church custodians drove by on our golf cart. (Don't you just love the golf-cart ministry?) He was just making the rounds, ensuring the safety of our group and our church. When we were done walking, most of the youth did not know who the guy on the golf cart was. I again asked how many people prayed for him. Everyone raised their hands. But here is where this story gets really interesting. The very next morning as I was making my way to my office, I ran into this cus-todian. He knew from previous weeks that we had been going into the community on Thursday mornings to help organizations and people who might need some assistance. He told me that his dad had cancer and that he was going through chemo. My friend, the custodian, was taking on other responsibilities to help his dad out, but had not had a chance to get over and clean up the yard, you know, little things like mowing and trimming hedges. He asked if we would be willing to go there on one Thursday morn-ing. I assured him we would. The next time we met as a group, I reminded them of the man in the golf cart. I told them who he was, and that he had requested our help. And the very next week we took about twenty youths over there and cut the grass, trimmed the hedges, swept, and even did some touch-up painting on the trim. Something so small that meant so much to a son and his dad. Imagine that. We prayed for this man, and then we had the opportunity to meet a practical need in his life. I could be wrong, but that seems to be the very thing that Jesus wants us to be doing. Just a thought.

When we returned to the church, everyone found the exercise exhilarating. One of the youth prayed, thanking the Lord that we were not stuck in some room *talking about* prayer, but rather how exciting it was that we were actually outside *praying*! Everyone prayed, and everyone began to catch a glimpse of the larger world that exists around them. Take a lesson from what one of our teenagers told us: We need to be in the act of praying, not merely talking about prayer in church. That is how lives will be changed, how this world will be transformed, how our lives will be filled with power and passion for the glory of God. I love how E. M. Bounds says that "through prayer we can take hold of God." [3]

The idea behind the prayer walk is to do exactly what one youth identified in his prayer—that is, to get beyond sitting in a cozy room talking about prayer, and move into the world around us with the spirit and activity of prayer. This allows God to open our eyes to so many people and things that we had once ignored, intentionally or not. This allows us the opportunity to see the community next to us with the eyes of God, to feel it with the heart of God, and to share a burden to seek change, restoration, and reconciliation in the name of Jesus Christ.

The first step is to see the community around you. For too long many Christians, and churches (don't worry—I definitely include myself here) have ignored the reality of communities in need. I don't know if we are scared, intimidated, have a misunderstanding about our role as Christians, or what. But what I do know is that God desires healing, restoration, reconciliation, unity, and community that extends beyond racial and economic boundaries. And if the church—those who know and follow Jesus Christ, are not willing to step out, then there will be no amount of government or any other aid that will create significant and lasting change.

Not too long ago we had two women come and speak to our youth. They shared about their experience of moving into a community fraught with drugs and neglect. And they shared how in the course of two years, probably some 90 percent of the drug activity has disappeared. Streets where families were afraid to come out of their homes are now filled with the laughter of children playing outside. While the issues are complex, the fact remains that change came to this community as these women began praying while they engaged the people. God has proved again to be stronger than drugs when faithful people exercise their faith.

PRAY WITH YOUR EYES WIDE OPEN

So how do you have a successful prayer walk? Simple. You get a group of people and walk around the community and pray. You can pray out loud or in silence. You can give them a passage of Scripture to focus on or just turn them loose. You can even get in a van and drive around the city. When our group went to San Francisco for a mission trip with The Center for Student Missions that was the first thing we did.[4] We drove around in silence for two hours just observing the city and praying for the people. In that short amount of time we saw things we would never have seen and quickly felt challenged and inspired to minister in the name of Jesus with all our energy for that week. It is because we *saw,* and in seeing our hearts became heavy for the people and city. Whatever you do, give your people the opportunity to see the community. Pray with your eyes *open*! See who you pass, and you will see the need. And may God bless you with a burden for your community like you have never had.

PRAYING THE SCRIPTURES

Recently we asked our group how many of them like to pray. Only a few raised their hands. When asked why not, we got many of the expected responses. "It is too hard." "I don't really understand prayer." "I don't ever feel like God hears my prayers." "I don't know what to pray for." And the list goes on and on and on. So I asked how they would feel if I guaranteed that they would never have to worry about what to pray again? What if you never had to wonder if God was listening, or whether you were praying a powerful and effective prayer? Would that give you more confidence in prayer? It sure would give me more confidence.

So here is what you do. You learn to pray through the Scriptures. There are many advantages to this. There are thoughts in the Bible on virtually every situation we face. You find honest, impassioned pleas before God from the people of God, who serve as great models for prayer. But perhaps the most compelling reason that I have found is this—when you pray the Scriptures you are praying the very heart of God! And if you are praying the heart of God, you can be sure that God will listen and respond.

Praying the Scriptures can help us not to pray out of selfish ambition, but rather to mold our hearts and minds to the heart and mind of God. Psalm 37:4 states that God will give us the desires of our hearts. I have long thought that there should be a phrase added to the end of that, because so many people have come to misuse that statement and then blame God when they believe their prayers go unanswered.

> Praying the Scriptures can help us not to pray out of selfish ambition, but rather to mold our hearts and minds to the heart and mind of God.

Maybe it is better understood expressed like this, "God will give you the desires of your heart, *when the desires of your heart are God's desires for you.*" Praying the Scriptures helps shape the desires of our hearts into God's desires for us. Again, the result is we will be praying the heart of God with lasting and effective prayers. Traditional worship services do this very well. If you are unsure of this, open a hymnal. There are numerous opportunities for a variety of occasions. Many hymnals have responsive reading and prayers from Scripture. This is one way of engaging your people and teaching them to pray. Do more responsive readings in worship. Find more passages that relate to the topic of study. I just don't think you can ever go wrong praying straight from the word of God.

PRAYER LABYRINTH

Some time ago prayer labyrinths began to take on some popularity. Honestly, I never really got this. I guess the Gregorian chant music accompanied by walking in a circle that took you nowhere just didn't seem too appealing to me. I was not too excited about this prayer labyrinth exercise. So we did what any creative person would do. We tweaked it a bit. It would be good of me to interject at this moment, if you haven't already figured this out, that tweaking is a good thing. The Holy Spirit can work through tweaking. We wholly advocate the necessary tweaking of anything that we offer for the sake of speaking to and reaching people for the cause of Jesus Christ. In other words, just tweak it!

We used the maze given to us, which took up the entire fifty foot by fifty foot room that we had. We set the candles all over the place to create the desired mood. However, the only change we made and, in our opinion, what made it work, was the music. Now, I must make it very clear that I have nothing specifically against Gregorians. So we created a montage of various contemporary artists focusing on reflective, thought-provoking lyrics that pierced the heart and soul with the majesty and awe of our Holy God.

As it turned out, the tweaking worked for our group. It connected. People were engaged. I know several people who were dealing with very heavy issues and decisions who seemed to grasp some clarity or direction as a result of centering on Jesus through this exercise. I know this was powerful because my wife and I were really wrestling with a touchy decision about our occupational future. We both felt a sense of God's presence and direction during this time, and it helped shape our decision to remain where we were. So God met us and others in this place once again. Beautiful.

PRAYER EXPERIMENTS

Another fun thing to do is to incorporate prayer experiments into worship. At different times in my ministry, I have invited people to journey on thirty-day prayer experiments. I like to call them experiments because there is no way to determine what exactly is going to happen when you begin the journey. You just have to go for it and see where God leads and where God shows up. It is quite an adventure. One such experiment that I think is fun is to invite people who are interested to sign their name on a piece of paper—like taking roll. Everyone signs the same paper.

This might become difficult with a really large group, so you might have to tweak it. You might have to try it in groups, of fifteen to thirty. Make photocopies of the paper for everyone. For the next thirty days ask everyone to be intentional about praying for each name on the list. I know what you are thinking right now. "Shouldn't we be praying for everyone, everyday, anyway?" Yes, but this allows for more intentional, focused praying rather than the obligatory blanket prayer—God, please bless our entire congregation. It should be rather exciting for the group over the next month to talk about what God is doing in their lives, or how they are sensing God's presence, or where they feel God is leading them.

Another great experiment comes from our good friend and author Terry Esau. He wrote a book entitled *Surprise Me: A 30 Day Faith Experiment* (Colorado Springs, Colo.: NavPress, 2005). It is his journey into seeking God in the everyday things, of just waking up and praying, "Surprise me, God," with no other agenda. This is a great experiment to try with your church. Grab the book. Have Terry come share at your church. Turn your people loose to pray and invite God to invade their lives. But here is the kicker. Give your people a chance to share at church. Pastors, be willing to release the pulpit for a Sunday, or dare we suggest a whole month, and let the church share how they have experienced God. I know this is risky, but I fully believe that God is capable of speaking through someone other than *you*. Give it a try. Besides, wouldn't it be nice to have a break? This is the perfect excuse. So go! Pray! And share what God has done! I have always believed the best stories are the ones that are born from within our own churches. Let the stories come forth.

CONCLUSION

A couple years back, we had yet another crisis in the Sorensen house. Our cat of eight years turned up missing after we had just relocated to another city to start a new position at a church in Tyler, Texas. Now there is something you must know about Charlie, our twenty-pound black cat: he has used *all* nine lives *and* is currently somewhere on life number twenty-two. He has suffered abscesses; fights with stronger, less spoiled cats; and even a three-minute tumble in the dryer (he since learned from that one that the dryer is not a good place to bunk at night before morning laundry chores begin again).

Back to the story. We had just moved, and Charlie went out one afternoon and didn't come back. Days turned into weeks and weeks eventually turned into a month and everyone in the house was quickly losing hope that we would ever see Charlie again; that is, everyone except for Nicholas. Nicholas, my now twelve-year-old, would not accept that Charlie was gone and every night during prayers, he prayed with such passion, "And dear Lord, *please* bring my Charlie back to me." I remember several times coming out and asking my wife, "How do I tell Nicholas that Charlie is not coming back?" I pondered that for several nights until the one night we received the call. It was from a teacher friend of my wife who asked if we were missing "a rather large black cat." She said that her neighbors *across town* were renovating their home and there was a stray black cat under the house that the workers had been trying to catch but were unable to. She thought maybe it was ours.

I remember laughing at that thought, but we both thought a visit would be worth the effort. So, the next day we loaded up and took a trip to the house across town. We looked around for a few minutes, and then I gazed under the house to see the glare of cat eyes staring back at me. Could this really be Charlie? After several attempts to get him to come to us, he didn't, so I had one last idea that I liked to call, OPERATION: ARCHIBALD. Now Archibald would be our *other*, twenty-two-pound cat (we grow healthy animals) and my thought was this: Charlie and Archibald were buds so we would go home, leash up Archibald and bring him back to see if there would be any love between the two. So we went home, leashed up the Arch, and brought him back to the house. I dropped him in front of the opening under the house, and then it happened. Archibald caught a glimpse of the black cat and arched up his back and went into attack stance—then we all watched as he relaxed as the two cats just came nose to nose and loved on each other. It was at that time that we knew—Charlie was found.

The best part of all of this came when we brought Charlie back home. It was so amazing to me that we had found him some month and a week later, and he was back in our home (needless to say, he doesn't wander out much anymore). After making mention of this to my wife, Nicholas came up to me and grabbed my leg and said the following: "See Dad, God *did* hear my prayer, and Charlie is back home."

At that point I found it hard to swallow. It brought me back to his nightly prayer where he boldly prayed, "Please God, bring Charlie back to me." Now this is important to understand. I don't share this story to imply that *whatever* you pray, God will grant it. Odds are, if you fervently pray for the primo parking spot at Target, the parking lot will *not* mysteriously part for you. What I do get from this story is *children* get it. And Jesus *recognized* this concept. In a moment where the disciples were shooing the kids away, Jesus responded with, "Let the little children come to me, and do not hinder them, for the kingdom of heaven belongs to such as these" (Matthew 19:14 NIV). What is it that kids have that we as adults lose? Passion. Boldness. And what would the *prayer-filled life* look like if we prayed *believing* God would actually hear and respond? Good news, my friends: prayer works. God awaits, so what are you waiting for? And what better place to encounter God than in worship?

CHAPTER 5

RECLAIMING THE POWER OF WORSHIP THROUGH STUDY

The word of God, well understood and religiously obeyed, is the shortest route to spiritual perfection. And we must not select a few favorite passages to the exclusion of others. Nothing less than a whole Bible can make a whole Christian. —A. W. Tozer

Scripture says that we have been given the mind of Christ. What an amazing thing to ponder, and one of the most practical ways this works itself out is through the study of the word. But what does it look like to study the word of God? Glad you asked. To study the word is to take a long, deep look into the heart of Christ. What we then extract, or, rather, have impressed upon us, is, in fact, the mind of Christ. It has been my observation lately that the study of God's word is becoming a lost art. Don't believe me? Ask around. I encounter more and more people on a daily basis who, when asked about their impression of God's word and its relevancy for them and their lives, it's almost as if they view the Bible as a book of laws and rules by which to oppress others and keep them from experiencing the joy and life that God intended. The tragedy in this thought process is that *nothing* could be further from the truth!

But, oh, how beautiful it is when we come to the Bible with an attitude that proclaims, "Teach me, oh God. Show me Your ways. For I am Your servant and I am listening."[1] When that occurs, when we, in our lives and the lives of our congregation, take on that approach to being open to receive what God has prepared for us, then we can truly be transformed into the likeness and image of Jesus. We truly receive the mind of Christ. And our transformation yields a message that we can then proclaim with a holy boldness throughout our lives and ministries. That message will then have substance and power because it was born from an encounter.

We are told in the second letter to Timothy that, "All Scripture is given by God and is useful for teaching, for showing people what is wrong in their lives, for correcting faults, and for teaching how to live right" (3:16). This is not a mandate to accuse and condemn people who are sinning. I think the power of this verse is much deeper than commonly expressed. Look at the context surrounding it. Paul is recounting to Timothy the difference between those who know and follow the teachings of God and those who choose to reject them. But before you think he is advocating the lifestyle of the Pharisees, he clarifies, or rather completes his intention. He says the "Holy Scriptures . . . are able to make you wise. And that wisdom leads to salvation through faith in Christ Jesus" (3:15). How beautiful is that? Yes, study the Scriptures, because they are able to offer wisdom. But be careful. Your wisdom is not only in your ability to quote passages, but it is rooted squarely in your capacity to accept the truth of Jesus Christ.

When grounded in this truth, the Scriptures come to life as they move and instruct you, and direct and challenge your worldviews. Ultimately the goal is that the person in Christ will be fully capable—having been transformed and given the mind of Christ—to accomplish the good works that God so desires for the people of this world. Yes, God desires holiness and right living, but we are to teach humbly and lovingly from what we ourselves have been shown through our own growth and maturing in Christ. We cannot blindly spout off rules and regulations with an expectation of compliance from those who don't yet know Christ. We are to gently, lovingly, with strong but humble authority point others toward Jesus through our actions. We spur others on from our own maturing wisdom. In this manner, as the letter to Timothy continues, we will be more than ready to have a defense for what we profess. This is true knowledge that is powerful and effective in the life of Christian witness, and the result of intentional and disciplined study.

TEACHING CONGREGATIONS TO STUDY THE WORD

I love the image story of John the Baptizer as revealed in the Gospel of John, the sixth chapter. You read about his death, but there is one sentence in there that reveals so much about his life. Remember in this story that King Herod is tricked into having John beheaded. He didn't want to because "he knew John was a good and holy man." The next sentence is even more interesting to me, and I believe this is how we should set about our preaching. The Bible says, "Also, though John's preaching always bothered [Herod], he enjoyed listening to John" (Mark 6:20). Our messages need to be about more than just behavior modification. They need to bring about life transformation that comes from a renewing of the spirit. **We don't need any more "How To" messages. We need more Father-centered, Jesus-elevated, Holy-Spirit empowered encounters with God through the Bible during worship.**

So my thoughts now turn toward this driving question: *How are we teaching our congregations to study the word?* I have heard that early on in the life of the church, when the people gathered to hear the "proclamation of the word," that is exactly what they got. They would sit with great anticipation and expectation as the leader moved to the front and opened the Holy Scriptures. And the reading of the Word of God would begin. The leader might begin reading in Romans 1:1. And he would read and read and read. Chapter 1 gone. But in its wake, a holy conviction is present among the mass of people who now realize that in their own ways, they too have traded the glory of God for the worship of powerless idols. The reading continues into chapter 2. And the people continue to squirm with delight as they are reminded that hearing the law alone is not what offers life and pleases God. Obedience is a strong and real necessity of right living, and the lack of obedience in the life of one who claims Christ shames the name of God and causes others to scoff at God. And so the reader reads. He continues on, allowing the word of God to be the word of God. Not seeking to add or detract by introducing or forcing preconceived perspectives of life onto the text. Maybe there is only time for the reading of four chapters, but by this time the people are ripe with anticipation of God's life-giving message. Those gathered to listen hear these words in conclusion, "God will accept us also because we believe in the One who raised Jesus our Lord from the dead. Jesus was given to die for our sins, and he was raised from the dead to make us right with God" (Romans 4:24-25).

In this moment, because God has been moving through the hearing of the word, people proclaim Christ in their lives because they have come to grasp the truth of their depravity along with the compelling grace of God in Jesus Christ! No twisting. No manipulating. No distortions. Just the raw, untamed word of God that points to the supremacy of Christ as the only hope for the world.

I know. It is a terrifying thought to just open the Bible in worship and read, and I can hear the objections now. "People sleep through my sermons." "How can anyone expect members of my congregation to stay awake if we just read the Bible?" But who then will explain what the text is really trying to say? What about all those stories (parables) where Jesus doesn't really mean what he says, but rather wants you to understand what he thinks you need to be thinking about—not what you actually are thinking about? Who is going to explain that if we just read the Bible? It is preposterous. Maybe some of you are just crazy enough to read these words and you are thinking, "That might be one of the coolest things to try." If you find yourself in that camp, blessings and peace be upon you. You will need it. I'm just kidding. Sort of.

It is important for me to add the following: I am not advocating the complete elimination of sermons as we know them today.

But I am challenging us as leaders in the church to engage the people of God in a variety of ways so the routine of church moves beyond routine. In our own church setting, we decided to give this radical concept a try. Now we put our own little spin on this study experiment, but I thought it would be fun. Naturally some were skeptical about the idea, but we really wanted to give this idea a try. So here is what we proposed. We suggested that we have absolutely no music. None. We simply gathered the people into the room, sat them down, said an opening prayer, and began reading from the Bible. The hope was that at any point during the reading of the word, anyone could interrupt if they had a question, comment, or concern about what they heard.

Did you catch that? We were asking those present on that evening to interrupt the reading at any point to seek clarification or to just make an observation. What on *earth* were we thinking? Can I just say that it is my fervent prayer and hope that every congregation has a child like Jenna. Jenna is the very reason my palms sweat whenever I have the joy of doing our children's message in worship service. Why? Not because she is a bad or unruly child, it is just that, well, she is vocal, honest, loud, and proud to be five years old. She is unpredictable, and she says whatever is on her mind. We need more people in the church like Jenna. Is it really a bad thing to desire more knowledge? Especially when it comes to God?

Honestly? We go to great lengths to make sure that the worship service and the sermon are not interrupted. But an opportunity to read Scripture and let it stand alone for an evening worship service sounded like a loaded opportunity for fun. I must be totally honest; some members of our worship planning team were not quite so sure this would work. Understandably, they were a bit hesitant to spend an entire evening just reading. How many people struggle with personal reading times? So many complain that it is hard to read the Bible. It is too difficult to understand. It is outdated. It is boring. But in the spirit of this Wednesday evening service we were involved in, God delivered through *praise* and *prayer*, so why doubt Him on the topic of Scripture? We proceeded with joyful but nervous anticipation for the time of worship without music.

Here is how we set up our evening contemporary service dealing with "study." We took one of the rooms in the church, a large room, and transformed it into the likeness of a living room. Aside from the size being a bit larger than average, it was quite a cozy little place by the time we finished. We moved in all sorts of couches from the youth area. We brought lamps from all over the place. We hung paintings. We even hung makeshift curtains to give it that extra homey feel. We would have put a fireplace in there, but previous experiments with fire kept this suggestion at bay. We laid rugs all over the floor and threw down huge floor pillows for people to spread out on. Comfy. Cozy. Homey. All the ingredients for a nonthreatening time of studying the Bible. The people gathered. We set up the service, explaining what was to happen. The invitation was to open Bibles and follow along. Mark prayed using the words of the Matt Redman song "The Heart of Worship." And we were off.

I turned to the book of Colossians and began reading in chapter 1, verse 1. About a minute into the reading, one of the brave souls in the youth group raised her hand and blurted out, "Is this what we are supposed to do? Just interrupt with our question? Because I have a question about verse 5." Beautiful. For the next hour and a half we read, asked questions, sought answers, discussed, debated, searched the Scriptures, and began reading again. Would you believe it?

We made it through an entire fifteen verses of the first chapter in the book of Colossians! It was so much fun. We had eleven- and twelve-year-old kids not afraid to ask whatever question came to their minds. I recall at one point we were talking about servants and lords. One of the younger kids asked what a lord (not Jesus) was. From there we actually had about a five-minute history lesson about cultures—how there were people who ruled (lords) over other people (servants or slaves) and how that culture influenced and affected the context of Scripture. What a great teaching moment for this young person. Not only did she learn something about the culture of the Bible and its people but also something about social class systems that eventually she will study in school. The time of study was spent moving all throughout the Bible. We had cultivated an environment where everyone was comfortable asking whatever question they had.

We journeyed into deeper theological issues, the nature of God, social issues that we struggle with in our society today, and so much more. After it was all over, we took a poll online to ask people which of the four evenings of worship they enjoyed the most: the service of prayer, praise, study, or communion. By about a three-to-one count, study was the favorite. Who would have thought just opening the Bible and letting it speak to us through honest examination and conversation with others would be sufficient to engage and satisfy the spiritual desires of people?

It is important for me to add this thought. While we were teaching at a conference in Oklahoma, sharing many of the thoughts in this book, we shared about this night of study. When we took some questions, one lady spoke up and said she thought it was a dangerous way to lead because of the potential for a bunch of ignorant people to spout off a bunch of ignorant thoughts about God. (Please know that by *ignorant* I mean a simple lack of knowledge. My father always told me ignorance could be cured—stupidity was forever.)

The people in our churches are not stupid, although some may be ignorant—without knowledge—of certain things about the Bible. (This is what the lady was referring to.) This will not serve to educate people but rather to make things worse because instead of growing in our understanding of biblical knowledge, we are potentially growing in our ignorance. We acknowledged the value in her comment. There is truth there. But what is the risk of not offering people a chance to learn and share together? What are the long-term effects of not allowing people to struggle through the Scriptures, to wrestle with the texts in an effort to gain understanding? I believe that too often we as leaders just spoon-feed people morsels of truth because either we don't think they can handle the full meal, or we ourselves are not prepared to give it to them. I must be honest. I will not forget that evening that we solely let the word of God stand on its own, and it did, and in a powerful way!

Another example of letting the Scriptures speak for themselves was on a high school retreat I recently led. I gave each student a letter in the New Testament to study for the week. Throughout the week, I told them, they were going to have opportunities to share what they were discovering about God, about life, about themselves, or anything else they uncovered. Basically speaking, they were going to be doing the teaching for the retreat; not me. Many of them initially seemed intimidated by the prospect of having to teach the Bible or lead a Bible study.

Most had never been placed in that position. So I gave them a list of basic questions to ask about the text, you know, things like who wrote the book? To whom was it written? Is there a particular issue that is being addressed? Why was it written? What are some recurring words, ideas, or themes? Where else in the Bible do you see these themes, ideas, or words? What do you like most in the book? Least? What was challenging? Was there anything you did not understand? What did you discover about Jesus? What does the text teach you about the nature of God, your world, and yourself? What do you want the group to take from your study?

So off we went, having a great time of laughter and fun throughout the week with the knowledge that the students were going to be the leaders. When it came time to share, I encouraged them that this was a time of learning together, that no one needed to feel that their efforts were any less than someone else's. It was so much fun to see what they uncovered. Through the nervousness of the experience, several students shared with me that this was the first time they had ever spent that much time alone with the Bible. Several others shared with great excitement that they were capable of discovering something about God on their own through the study of God's word. And still others told me they enjoyed it so much that in the future, they would like to have more opportunities to lead studies or teach from the Bible to their peers.

One student asked me, "Does it always feel like that?" I clarified, "Do you mean feel good when teaching?" "Yes!" he said. With a large smile on my face I replied, "When you have discovered something new about God that you want everyone to know, yes. It does." This is exactly what I hoped would occur. I was less interested in what they uncovered than I was in God stirring within the students a desire to seek God more through the Bible. What they needed was a place and time to search (the retreat), with some guidance (questions), and then the opportunity to share what they discovered (teaching moments). Since the retreat I have called on several of them to lead during our regular youth gatherings, and they have done a fantastic job. It is my hope and prayer that they will continue to grow in their passion for the word of God, and that their studies will yield opportunities to share with others.

Another example of letting Scripture stand on its own came in the form of a college retreat I once led. I found myself in a precarious position as I did not have a worship leader to go with me, and though I think my singing can be compared to that of a blend of Michael Bublé and Tony Bennett, my wife quickly brings me back to reality and encourages me to keep my vocal gifts confined to the shower. So what to do? I used the psalms. Each evening when we had our worship and devotion, I had a student open up to Psalm 1 and read. We let the Scriptures *be* the music of our hearts, and by day three, the students could not get enough of what they were reading. Again, how simple a thought but how powerful it was for us on that trip!

So what is the lesson in this? Maybe one lesson is simply this: sometimes I think we overcomplicate how we try to communicate the truths of the Bible. I think we would all agree that there have been times when we have not had something new to say about the Bible, but we have forced a sermon through because that is what we are supposed to do. I also think there are times when we feel no one else can preach or teach in our place, so even though we are completely spent, exhausted, or battle weary, we continue to force ourselves forward, thinking we will be OK, and that our efforts honor God and will bless others. The truth is that we as pastors and leaders in the church need to recognize when we need to step away, to retreat, and relax. We should be *models* of that!

I can't tell you how many sermons I have heard pastors preach that outline steps to personal care and nourishing of the soul that specifically include taking time to get away and regroup. Unfortunately many of those pastors that have preached that thought have neglected to follow their own advice. We must teach with the intent of raising others up, and then give them opportunities to lead and teach in various ways. Not only does it give us as leaders opportunities to take needed breaks, it builds up the church of Jesus Christ by offering those in our congregations opportunities to stretch their spiritual wings and take on more responsibility in leading others.

Let us remember that each person is called to minister and that there are plenty of gifts for all. Having a degree and being ordained does not necessarily entitle or gift you for preaching and teaching. Your gifts may lie in counseling, or executive type roles such as administering, overseeing others, and raising finances to support the ministry. Maybe your passion is organizing and leading mission opportunities. Maybe the main thing you do is care for the church in various ways. And just maybe God has placed the gifts that you lack as a minister in others within your congregation. If we are effectively studying the word of God, and leading others into powerful study while teaching them how to study, then I confidently believe that the Lord will plant in the hearts of people the desires to effectively minister to the whole of the church. God will raise up (through our leadership and teaching) people who can supplement our weaknesses. Rather than feel threatened by their strengths, let us joyfully accept them and encourage them with opportunities to lead—including teaching and preaching.

So, church, let us study the word of God in order that we may show ourselves approved unto God. Let us find and experience the risen Christ in the midst of the Scriptures. Let us create opportunities to take others into the joy-filled journey of reading the Bible.

> Listen, people of Israel! The LORD our God is the only LORD. Love the LORD your God with all your heart, all your soul, and all your strength. Always remember these commands I give you today. Teach them to your children, and talk about them when you sit at home and walk along the road, when you lie down and when you get up. Write them down and tie them to your hands as a sign. Tie them on your forehead to remind you, and write them on your doors and gates. —Deuteronomy 6:4-9

CHAPTER 6

RECLAIMING THE POWER OF WORSHIP THROUGH COMMUNION

" 'Go out quickly into the streets and alleys of the town and
bring in the poor, the crippled, the blind and the lame.'

'Sir,' the servant said, 'what you ordered has been done,
but there is still room.'

"Then the master told his servant, 'Go out to the roads
and country lanes and make them come in, so that my house
will be full.' "
—Luke 14:21-23 NIV

What is it about teenagers that they have absolutely *no
trouble* telling you what they think? Trust me when I
say that after nine years of youth ministry, I learned
to both fear and appreciate the free spirit of what is known as the
teenager. Allow me to explain.

A couple of years ago, I got an opportunity to speak at a youth
district training event to young people who were the leaders in

their youth groups and churches. I took the ninety minutes I was given to talk about the Scriptures and challenged the youth to take this holy, God-breathed, divine revelation given to us through Scripture and make it the focus of their youth gatherings. It will always amaze me that we have this book called the Bible and, oftentimes, we spend so much time grabbing easy put-together devotionals and preach our own issues and agendas rather than let the Scriptures speak for themselves. Really. How can the word of God be boring?

That rant was free, and now back to the story. I gave them different Scripture passages: Moses and the burning bush, Elijah encountering God, Jesus and the communion passage, to name a few. Then I threw out the challenge to "get creative." The question was, "How can you, in a creative way, bring those stories to life using the five senses, and share with me what you would do?" Man, did I ever get some creativity. Take the story of Elijah, for example. Remember the passage where he is on the mountain after having a pity party and whining to God (by the way, if whining was a fruit of the spirit, I would meet my vitamin C quota on a daily basis). He desires to see God and God shows Himself to Elijah. But it is not in the wind or earthquake or fire; it is in the still, small voice.

Now, how could you bring that passage to life? The teenagers on that Saturday afternoon shared with me some terrific thoughts. Some of my favorites were in the form of bringing vacuum cleaners into the worship space with strobe lights. As the scriptures were read, they recommended flashing the lights of the worship area and turning on the vacuum cleaners and letting the chaos ensue. And when Elijah encounters God in the silence they would hit the off switch. Beautiful, huh? (I can just see our ushers at First Church,

Shreveport, getting the dry vacs and standing around the congregation just letting them rip some *mighty* wind on the people. Now *that* is a service that excites me!) Needless to say, the creativity ensued and there was a lot of sharing, but one of my favorite moments that afternoon came on the topic of communion.

GETTING ENOUGH JESUS

We were talking about this beautiful act of breaking the bread and tasting the wine and how you could share together in that service in a different, creative way. As the discussion on communion ensued, sparks were popping and creativity was flowing when, all of the sudden, a child stood up and raised his hand. I will never forget his passion. I called on him and he shared the following: "Can I just say that I have a problem with communion in my church?" At this moment, the room fell quiet and the attention of everyone there that day fell on my new friend. I asked him to go on and he gave the following statement: "The problem I have is that I just don't *ever* get enough Jesus."

This caught me off guard and I wasn't quite sure where to go with this so I asked for a little more explanation. Without a single pause in his breath, he followed with, "*I don't get enough Jesus!* They pinch off this tiny piece of bread and that is all I get. When I come down to receive, *I want me some Jesus*! Break me off a *chunk* and let me be *filled!*" A thunder of applause and amens followed that comment. I laugh now thinking of the youth who went to receive communion that following Sunday and looked at their preacher and responded, "I'm sorry, is that all? I don't think so!" [grabs a bigger chunk of Jesus, and runs off].

So, as our worship team approached a service in our church that dealt solely with the theme of communion, we sat down and looked at a couple of passages from the Bible. The first was from Luke 14, which started this chapter. If you haven't read it, put the book down and find it. I love this passage. Honestly? I can't tell you I have ever heard this one preached before in relation to the topic of communion. In the scripture, Jesus is eating, no wait, *communing* at the home of a Pharisee who says to Him, "Blessed is the man who will eat at the feast in the kingdom of God" (Luke 14:15 NIV). (Point—Pharisee.) I love Jesus' response to this comment. He basically says, "Yeah, about that. A man was preparing a great banquet and sent his servant out to tell all he sees to come, 'for everything is prepared.' The servant does not have an easy job as he meets excuse after excuse. One says, 'I have to tend my field.' Another says, 'Wow, thanks for the invite, however, I just bought five yoke of oxen and I need to break them in. Sorry.' (Coincidentally, I used the same yoke excuse to get out of a college exam; the professor didn't buy it, either.) Yet another excuse went like this, 'I just got married. Sorry.' " (OK, let's be honest. This might be the only acceptable excuse. Come on, Jesus. Newly married? "You've got to let me go. You don't know my wife.") So the servant reports back to the master who meets this news with the following request. He immediately tells the servant to "go out quickly into the streets and alleys of town and bring the poor, the crippled, and the blind and lame." The servant obeys without question and when this is done, he reports back with the news that there is still room, to which the master responds with the command to go out to the roads and country lanes and invite *even more* to the table.

I love this passage! Can't you just see the scene? You can just see the decorated banquet hall. In the center of the hall you will find a table with enough chairs for all who have gathered. And you look on the table and before you is food enough for everyone who has come; a feast beyond all imagination. And as if *that* is not enough, it gets better. Who is sitting around the table? "The poor, the crippled, the blind, and the lame." But wait, there is more. The HIV-infected, the homeless, the tax collector, and the prostitute. Next to them you see your neighbor, your pastor, Democrats, Republicans, and, what? Even Ralph Nader *next to* Al Sharpton! And then it registers. **All have the invitation to come and sit at the Master's table!**

And then there is the story of "Bo." You are familiar with this one, right? In 2 Samuel, chapter 9, we find King David, who has taken the throne of Israel after the death of King Saul, and his friend Jonathan. What I love about David is, time and time again, you see him continually wanting to *give back* to God because of the rich blessings God continually showers down on him. So in 2 Samuel 9:1 we find David asking these words, "Is there anyone still left of the house of Saul to whom I can show kindness for Jonathan's sake?" (NIV). Amazing. Here, at a time that kings would *intentionally* wipe out the lineage of former kings to assure none of the descendants would get the idea of over-throwing the kingdom, David wants to *bless* any of the descendants of Saul for Jonathan's sake.

Enter into the picture Mephibosheth, or "Bo" as I like to call him (you have to admit, "Bo" just rolls off of the tongue easier). When you read this passage, we hear from Ziba, who was from the household of Saul, who shares that there is someone left from the house of Saul and his name is Mephibosheth, the son of

Jonathan. But if you read the passage you find a very interesting point raised by Ziba in verse 3. He shares that, "There is still a son of Jonathan; he is crippled in both feet" (NIV). Translation: "Yes, Jonathan has a son but he has a disability. He's not worthy of any of your blessings, David. You wouldn't want *that* one sitting at your table." And how does David react to that news? "Bring him to me." The Scriptures say that "Bo" was living in a place called Lo Debar, which translates to "no pastureland"; he was *in hiding* in a dry, barren wasteland knowing that, at any point, the knock would come at the door and his life would be over.

Let me ask you, how many of us have been to that place in our lives? The church encounters the lost and afraid on a daily basis, not just within her walls but in the greater community as well.

Well, the day came that, indeed, there was a knock at the door and it was David's soldiers. Put yourself in the place of Mephibosheth riding with the guards on the road to David's palace. Imagine the thought of knowing that life was over and this would be the end. However, what he would find would be the very opposite of what he had expected. (Praise God!) The Scriptures say that he came into the palace and *bowed down* before David. Now, don't miss this amazing piece of the picture. Here is Mephibosheth, both of whose legs were disabled, making his way before the king and bowing down before the king. David says, "Get up," and then shares the good news: "From this day forward, you will eat all of your meals at my table." Beautiful. On that day, Mephibosheth found that death was not on the agenda, a *feast* was. A *place setting* was prepared at the king's table and the reservation was made for that night, and every following night for the remainder of Bo's life. This is, in my humble opinion, one of the most beautiful and honest pictures and definitions of the word *grace* you will find in the Old Testament.

So with those two Scripture passages in mind, our worship team began to prepare for a service that would deal with the theme of communion. In preparing our hearts for this adventure, God brought us to *fast*. I love how God works. In my personal study time of Scripture, I had been led to various passages where fasting was observed and I had shared with my group that maybe we needed to fast. I'll be honest, I was hoping they would respond with, "Nope. That is not what I am sensing, Mark." However, that is not the response I received. I got a resounding yes from the group. Thus, it began. On Tuesdays we, as a worship team, fasted from sunup to sundown, saying to God, "We just want to be completely open to your leading and your voice as we seek you out in this process." Isn't it amazing, by the way, when you truly put yourself out there to show God you are serious, God answers and answers loudly? On this particular service, however, we dared to imagine, *What if for this experience, we extended the invitation of fasting beyond our worship team, to the entire group attending that service?* So that is exactly what we did.

The week before our communion service, we shared how our worship team had been fasting for the sole purpose of hearing God speak. We then said that the following Wednesday we would be having communion with one another. We also asked the congregation to prepare their hearts for the service; we invited all who were attending to fast with us the following Wednesday from sunup to sundown. We didn't put unnecessary pressure on any of the youth or adults to do it, just threw out there the invitation to join us and see what God could say through this process of sacrifice.

So the following Wednesday, the people began to gather. And more than that, they had fasted: everyone who came that night. We found teenagers who had fasted (a great story we would later find out played out like this in a cafeteria: "Hey man. Want some of my chips?"

"No, thank you. I can't."

"You can't? Why not?"

"Well, if you must know, I am fasting."

"Fasting? Why are you doing that?"

"Beats me. All I know is that my youth director told me to." Obviously, a little more explanation was needed with this individual!)

We found parents who had fasted with their kids, college students who had fasted, *everyone* who gathered that night. And as they walked into the room, they were hungry; very hungry. Here is what they saw.

On the floor, we had set up several long tables surrounded by pillows. The tables were covered with a simple tablecloth and there were plates and cups as if it were set up for a meal. At the head of the table was an altar made up of a cross, and at the foot of the cross was a simple loaf of bread and a chalice with juice. Everyone gathered around the table and took their place. This is when we began with prayer and a reading of the Luke 14 passage.

We discussed briefly that night what it meant and set up the scene of the great banquet and feast that occurred, and we led the adults, the college students, the youth and all who attended into a prayer. It was funny. Thinking back, those in the room that actually saw the bread and juice were apprehensive because they wanted to *eat*! It wasn't enough food. To quote the child mentioned at the beginning of the chapter, they wanted them some

Jesus! We just assured them that we would be having communion with one another and there would be enough for everyone. That led us to the meat of the evening (no pun intended).

There are those moments in ministry (and I pray you have these) where you witness God leading and speaking in such a way that you can actually see the lightbulb go off and you realize that, for the first time, the worshipers get it. On this particular evening, we witnessed a group of people, all ages, who *got* what communion was all about. As we prayed with the group, volunteers snuck into the room and placed before all seated at the table baskets of fried catfish and bread that had been in the oven and were served warm. As the prayer finished and the amen was said, those seated at the table opened their eyes to see the "feast" before them.

I like to say that this *one* moment is one of my favorite ministry moments, as I will never forget the look on the faces of those there that night. You literally got light-headed in the room as the people had sucked so much oxygen out of the room upon seeing the meal that was before them. Priceless. Then came this pause, this holy hesitation like, *What do we do now?* We looked at them and said, "Welcome to the banquet. Let's feast." And that was all that was needed. The feast ensued. For over an hour and a half that night, our sermon on communion was a prayer and feasting on the meal that was on hand and laughing and sharing with one another. Now let me add at this point that there was no liturgy; no Great Thanksgiving and blessing of the elements *all of which are beautiful ways* of celebrating communion. At this particular service, simplicity overruled tradition and God blessed all who were there that night. I loved a question that came at the conclusion of the evening from a young girl named Camille. She came up to me awkwardly and asked the question, "Hey, when are we having communion?" This after the hour we had spent eating fish and bread. I just smiled and said back to her, "Camille, the feast *was* communion!" And the look on her face showing she understood? Absolutely priceless.

Thinking back on that evening, I am reminded that the surprises from God just kept on coming. As the people gathered for that evening service, we noticed a face present that night that we had not seen, and it didn't take long to notice he was a visitor. John introduced himself to us and his clothes were dirty and matted, and it was very clear that he hadn't had a meal in a long time. With our church being located where it is, we often have many homeless men and women who wander through our doors, and John, on that night, found his way up to the table. Isn't God amazing? One of my favorite memories will be the table that you see below. Seated around it were mothers and fathers, teenagers, college students, and children. And there, in the midst of them all was John. He wandered in that night and found himself, much like Mephibosheth, seated at the table worthy to feast with the king. And he was accepted and loved. Now come on, join me in a robust, "Praise God!"

Looking back at the Luke 14 passage historically, we cannot miss the point that Jesus is intentionally making. He is speaking to the Jewish people, the people of God. He is driving home the truth that God has called them as His holy people. They have been set apart, given a great honor in the kingdom of God. But they have not responded to that call. They have rejected the invitation of God. They have turned their backs on Him and made excuses for who they have become. They have misunderstood their calling and consequently kept others from experiencing the love and grace of God. So in this story, the story of Israel, God extends the invitation to *everyone*. He has sent forth into every valley and town that the rejects are now somebodies. The outcasts now have claim to the throne! They are no longer identified with their depravity. They are now identified with the Lord of all creation, the One who initiates and sustains life.

Now let's go back to the theme of "communion." Isn't this exactly what communion should be all about? Yes! It is remembering the sacrifice made for us by God through Jesus Christ. It is the invitation to the very least of people to dine with the King of kings. Those who have no right, no claim, are given the glorious privilege of *feasting* at the table of God. The lost are given opportunity to come home. Praise be to the God of infinite grace.

Now I raise the question, *How can this service look in your church?* The beautiful act of communion can happen in so many ways. Take your pick! I attended a college worship service recently, and for that morning, the speaker had cancelled and the director informed us that we would be reading from the Great Thanksgiving in our Methodist hymnals and this would serve as our devotion. It was beautiful, sweet, and fed my soul! That is one way.

Another thought comes in the form of what happened to us on the evening that we had encouraged our group to fast. Maybe your church is filled with souls willing to go further in their faith if just given the chance. What would it look like if you did a sermon series on communion and fasted *leading up to* a Sunday morning communion service in your church? Another great thought came in the form of a workshop we were leading where a pastor shared with us that she was extending an invitation to host a "Great Banquet" in her community taken from the Luke

14 passage and would use that as a way to feed *and* minister to those in her community. Let's be honest. The world is hungry and, sadly, they are choosing to feed from all of the wrong places. The greater question is, are we as the church prepared to give them the substance needed to sustain their spirit and soul? The table is prepared. Let the world come and take its place at the table!

I recently came across a prayer that was a part of the opening liturgy from the 19th World Methodist Conference held in Seoul, Korea. Let this prayer speak for us all:

> Bring quickly that new world
> where the fullness of your peace will be revealed.
> Keep us watchful for that day when
> people from every race, language and way of life
> will gather to share in the one eternal banquet with Jesus
> Christ our Lord.
> Through Him, in Him and with Him, in the unity of the Holy
> Spirit,
> all glory and honor is yours, almighty Father, now and forever.[1]

CHAPTER 7

BE WILLING TO FAIL

I like to think that the first *truly contemporary* worship service
you will find in the Gospels can be found in the book of
Matthew, chapter 14. Let me set the scene. Jesus had just finished feeding the five thousand and sent the disciples on ahead
of him while he snuck off for a little one-on-one time with his
Heavenly Father. Apparently the waves were a bit choppy that
evening because, as the Scriptures say, the boat had drifted a con-
siderable distance from the shore. So, being the kind Savior that
he is, Jesus *walks out* on the water to catch up with his friends.
Can anyone say "out of the box"?

As the disciples catch a glimpse of the figure on the water,
they are quick to jump to the idea of ghost, but Jesus responds
with a simple, "Take courage, it is I! Do not fear." Enter into the
scene, Peter. Oh, dear Peter. My wife likes to say that I share the
same character trait as Peter. If you could ask her what that
would be, she would simply smile, showing off that dimple, and
respond with, "You both speak before you think about what
is coming out of your mouth." And that is *exactly* what Peter
did in verse 28. "Lord, if it is you," Peter replied, "tell me to
come to you on the water." Now that is a great question. But

come on, do you *seriously* think he actually stopped to think that scenario out?

And then Jesus replied, "Come." I see the scene being played out as if frame by frame. The camera zooms in to Peter's face and a look of shock and dismay. "I'm sorry . . . did you just say 'Come'?" Slowly, ever so slowly, the camera moves out to reveal the other disciples who were hanging on to Peter when they thought Jesus was a ghost are *no longer standing* with Peter—they are on the other side of the boat giving Peter that encouraging, "Go get 'em, tiger," thumbs-up look. So, Peter steps out of the boat. Did you get that, church? He *stepped out of the boat.* He didn't form a small subcommittee of "in boat" disciples to write out the "what if" scenarios should this radical call from Christ not work. He actually listened, looked, and obeyed, fully taking into consideration that this call from Jesus was crazy, dangerous, and made absolutely no sense. And guess what happened? He took three steps and then sank.

Can you blame him? Give Peter some credit. He looks at Jesus, but assuming Peter had a touch of ADHD (again, I can relate), there were other factors to consider; wind, rain and, oh yes—he was *standing on liquid*! He sinks only to find Jesus is close by with a hand there to save him. Now here at this point in the story will determine whether you, my reader friend, are a "glass half empty" or a "glass half full" kind of person. You can look at Peter and say, "Wow, way to go, loser. You took that step of faith and you sank and you sank *hard*." Truthfully, I can see the disciples looking at Peter, nudging one another with smirks on their faces. But you know what? I can see Peter look them square in the eyes and respond with, "Hey, guess what? I took three steps on *liquid* today. How many did you take?" You go, Peter.

Church, it is time we listen to the voice of Christ and step outside of the boat and be *ready* for some opposition. I think any time a church is willing to be creative in worship, there will always be those who stand against it. Sometimes the opposition comes in the form of those outside the church as they laugh at our attempts to be relevant to the world. While words of discouragement might be frustrating, they are not the worst kind. The worst kind of opposition comes from within the church. There is nothing more deflating than to vision and pray for something, receive some direction about it, and then have it shot down or made fun of from those who are supposed to lift you up. Have any of you ever felt this?

Pastors, let's talk for a moment. Your God-ordained role as a pastor allows you the opportunity to be one of the most encouraging voices in the life of a dreamer. I am not only talking about those with ambition in the congregation but also those with courageous vision on your staff. Yes, listen to the creative ideas of your congregation, but be certain to listen and vision along with those hired and called by God—your staff members.

Sermons on reaching for your dreams or having a vision and pursuing it with a holy passion inspire congregations. There is no denying that such messages are the kind that move the congregation emotionally and spiritually. You hear the bustle and cheering of excitement at their conclusion. People walk out with joy and excitement about what is about to happen in their lives and in the life of the church. This is good, right? But what also tends to happen is members of the staff begin to share their wild and crazy ideas the next week or so in staff meeting. They heard your message, too! They actually listened to the sermon and are fully prepared to move in faith on what was preached from the pulpit.

Pastors, those leaders are stepping out of the boat. Are you going to take a step along with them? One of attentiveness and encouragement by offering your prayers, guidance, and trust? Or even an offer to journey with them, seeking clarity and fearlessness when the vision looks risky and goliath?

Dreams voiced by those under your leadership should be listened to and handled with the same care as you would give the congregation's. Be careful not to crush hopeful spirits with quick words such as, "It is never going to happen," or "We have to be realistic about things," or "Be bold? That message was for the congregation, not the staff." You have entrusted staff members to lead; let them lead. The challenge has been made to dream big for their ministry, for their families, for themselves; now let them share that dream with you, their messenger and pastor. Things may look or sound impossible, but it just might be the voice and direction of the God of all possibilities that they have heard. Read chapter 1 again. Fulfill your role. Did Jesus ever preach to the masses before him only to turn and proclaim to the disciples, "Sorry, this message of hope and my goodness is not for you"?

Go back to the prayer chapter. Remember the night of prayer where we invited everyone to engage in active praying for almost an hour? Right before we got started, and I mean five minutes before we got started, we actually were cautioned that we would run people away by asking them to pray for that long. We were told that three to five minutes was about the maximum time frame that people would be willing to give. After that they just lose focus and get bored. We were encouraged to reconsider and warned, "If you must go on with the long, extended prayer time, don't be surprised if you lose a lot of people." Needless to say, we pushed on with the expectation that God just might show up. And guess what? God did!

And then there was my own, personal, "Jesus, if it is really you tell me to come to you on the water" moment. I remember reading this incredible book a friend had given me and being so inspired by it that I emailed the author to tell him how much I loved what he had written. And within a day or so, he replied back with his cell phone number and we got an opportunity to talk. I remember just being so excited about the possibility of this guy coming and sharing with our congregation and the hopes of how it might jumpstart a prayer journey for our church. So I booked him.

Now, let me add that we don't have too many guest speakers come to our church, so we were excited about the service and who was coming. We blitzed the church with information about the event. We sent brochures to all the Sunday school rooms. We put posters up everywhere. We even made a couple of prominent displays about the coming opportunity. We redirected the youth ministry for this Sunday, and generally had great expectations all the way around. We were hoping to pack the theater where we meet. But here is the heart crusher. In the midst of all this excitement and energy, we had someone come and tell us not to get our hopes up too high. They told us that we would be lucky to have two-thirds of what we normally average on any given Sunday. They said that having a guest speaker was a good idea, but don't expect a big turnout. I remember hearing those words and responding with, "But I am dreaming big and expecting God to truly surprise us all!" The response? "Dreaming never hurt but you need to prepare yourself for reality." We continued on with the hope, and quite frankly with the expectation that God would be in the very middle of what we were doing. Would you believe it? It turns out that that Sunday was the single largest attended Sunday in the history of that particular worship service. You go, God! You can make anything happen. From that Sunday service many people in and out of the church enjoyed an ongoing prayer experiment that yielded many adventures and faith stories that I am still hearing about to this day.

GET VISUAL; GET CREATIVE

Let me also add that in stepping outside of the boat, we need to be prepared to splash the water around, and guess what, it just *might* get the sanctuary a tad wet (wait, is that an example I hear coming?). It is fun to work with visuals and hands-on things when shaping and leading a worship service. After all, how did Jesus teach the people he encountered? With parables; the modern-day equivalent of felt boards. We are a visual society today and really no different from the crowds that Jesus spoke to!

Once I borrowed the story from John Piper to teach about the danger of wasting our lives. It is the story of a couple who retired to Florida and spent their days collecting seashells, compared to that of two women who gave their lives and died for the cause of Christ in foreign missions. Which is the greater tragedy? Piper asks. The couple that will stand before the Lord and lift up their seashell collection; that is the greater tragedy.[1] As I shared this story and the weight of it sank in, I had a large basket of seashells that I dropped to the floor. They crashed hard and loud on the tile below and significantly startled everyone. Upon conclusion we invited everyone to grab a seashell in remembrance of not wasting our lives. Ninety percent of all the shells were picked up off the floor and mine remains in my office as a reminder of that evening.

And then there was the message I preached in our contemporary service on the desert. You know the desert, right? It is that place we *hate* because it is hot, uncomfortable, and most of the time it is that place where God is refining us and teaching us something. As I prepared for the service, Jamie, part of our contemporary service team, asked me my thoughts for putting the stage together for that particular Sunday. Without hesitation I said, "Jamie, I believe God wants sand poured all over the stage so when I preach on the desert, I can actually preach *from* the desert." This is what I love about Jamie. He looks at me, takes a deep breath, and then responds, "Are you *sure* that is God's voice talking to you?" That Sunday, people arrived to find a huge, barren desert on the worship stage, and it was an amazing service. I preached on the passage where God told Moses to take off his shoes, for the place he was standing was holy ground. And then I invited those in the congregation who were willing, to take off their shoes and come and join me and claim their place in the desert, acknowledging that God was in control. It took the song "Blessed Be Your Name" to a whole new level.

Finally, there was the sermon on Mary and Martha. You remember this one, right? Jesus shows up, and Martha is so busy getting the work of the house in order while Mary just sits at the feet of Christ? I gave this message on Mother's Day, and again, Jamie asked for direction as to how to set up the worship stage. I shared that I wanted half of the stage in disarray and the other half organized, clean, and set simply for worship. The purpose of the sermon was for mothers but also for anyone there who had become so distracted with compulsions and to-do lists and forgotten that Jesus and our relationship with the Father should be central to our lives.

You have to know that I have utmost confidence in my friend Jamie, and I really have no clue what the worship stage looks like *until Sunday morning.* On this particular Sunday morning, I was in for a shock, however. I arrived to find that Jamie had done *exactly* what I had asked for, but did he ever get carried away. Half of the worship stage was, indeed, beautiful and serene with a cross, kneeling rails, and color. The other half of the stage? A total mess! There were laundry baskets thrown around, unfolded clothes and empty pizza boxes scattered on the floor with (here is the big one) beer and wine bottles lying on the floor and book-shelves. *That* was what I was not prepared for. I was horrified, actually. "OK, beer and wine bottles have no place on our worship stage," I thought, so I quickly removed them and went about the preparations I had for that morning. And then the Holy Spirit began to speak to me. I began to hear the words I told Jamie. "This service is about our compulsions and what keeps us from encountering the Father." Alcoholism is just that. So, I made a deal with God. I basically said, "Look, I will take all of the bottles off the stage but one and let You guide the hearts and eyes that need to see that liquor bottle to it." Again, the service was quite powerful; and afterwards, there were three souls who mentioned the alcohol bottle and their need to get help, as that was a distraction to their life. Praise God!

Mark: At many conferences when we speak, Derek and I often are asked how we get the ideas for services and themes and where those come from. Easy answer here; pay attention to Christ's voice speaking around you!

Derek: I can recall that there was one entire year that Mark and I were constantly being shown the same things in Scripture about where we were supposed to lead. We would meet at a local coffee shop to pray about the direction we wanted to go for the next couple of months and both of us had brought the visions that we felt God had laid on our hearts to talk about and see where to place our emphasis.

Once, we discovered that we were reading the exact same book, and in fact we were in the exact same chapter (I think we were about three pages off). We compared notes (we both underline and write in the margins) to discover that we had noted virtually the same stories and points along several of the chapters. And let me add that I am not making any of this up. I promise! Now, I like to say that (insert your own Forrest Gump voice here) "I'm not a really smart man" but that just could be the voice of God a-speakin'! So we could not help thinking that maybe God was directing us to share some of what we were uncovering about life through the pages of this book. Done. We obeyed and had a marvelous six-week study that was ripe with the power and presence of God.

As we met and prepared for another series, this is what we found. I had been praying and seemingly not getting any clear direction. The only thing that kept coming into my mind was "name of God." This repeated a number of times, to which I kept responding to God, "YHWH." I guess I was telling God, "I know Your name. I have read it in the Bible. What else do You have? Where do You want us to go? How do You want us to study and pursue You these next weeks?" The only answer I got was "name of God." What do you do? So I went to meet with Mark only to discover that he had been in the bookstore about a week earlier and saw a book on praying the names of God. He thought it looked interesting so he bought it and had been reading through it. Imagine that.

I am not too bright a person, but it seemed obvious that maybe God wanted us to take a look at how God reveals Himself through His names. We had a glorious time looking at how God reveals Himself through six names in the Old Testament. We had banners made for each name of God. Each banner had the Hebrew name on top and the English translation beneath it. We hung them all around to remind us throughout the series that God's name reveals something specific about His character and nature and how He is willing to engage and influence our lives. We did a bunch of little things like putting adhesive bandages all around when we talked about God being our Healer. When we talked about the Lord as our Banner, we had a huge sheet up front that everyone could come and sign their name on or write something if they desired. We had it taped to a retractable screen and at the end of the service, we raised the screen. As we sang the closing song, the banner was lifted up. We raised a banner to the Lord and we were reminded that God is watching over us with love and protection.

One of the most beautiful things that occurred was a challenge that Mark took on. He felt strongly impressed by God to write a new song for each of the six names of God. What emerged were six absolutely beautiful and powerful works of art that took us to the throne of God's love and helped us grasp the nature of God as it was revealed in His name. One specific song I fell in love with has turned out to be a song we sing a lot in our worship services is "Provide." [2] It was written on behalf of a prayer to God as our *Provider*. I will never stop being amazed at how some of the most powerful songs come from the simplest of lyrics:

We want to see You, Lord. We want to feel you in this place. We want to hear You, Lord. We want to see Your face. Provide, Lord, take this life, deliver me. Provide, Lord, take this heart and captivate me. Provide for me.

And then there is "Heal Me, Lord":[3]

Broken I come to this place. Suffering in need of grace. Tired of feeling the shame, and hurting from all of this pain. I want to be healed, I want to be made aware. Take Your hands, Lord, and won't you please, hold me there. Heal me, Lord.

Amazing what God can say when we just give Him enough time to speak!

And then for us United Methodists, there is the *Book of Discipline* (how is that for a segue!?). The *Book of Discipline* is the book revised by the United Methodist General Conference that contains basic beliefs of the Church and defines how our faith meets our daily life. Now if I were forced to be honest here, I would have to say that I would prefer to avoid any book on policy and most types of discipline. But I understand they serve their purposes. I found myself reading the United Methodist *Book of Discipline* to prepare for some meetings that I had. And do you know what I discovered? (This is a classic case of ignorance being remedied.) I discovered that the statements of belief within the *Discipline* are profoundly rich with the power of God and rooted solidly in the Scriptures.

Before you say what many others have said about me and make fun of me in my blatant state of ignorance, consider how many others in your churches may be in the same position as I was. I would venture to say that hardly any average church attendee has read and knows how deep and how rich are the statements of faith as expressed in our *Discipline*. Here is where I am going with this. We thought it would be fun to spend a couple of months revisiting the basic tenets of our faith, and the *Discipline* unexpectedly provided exactly the direction we were looking for. It was so beautifully laid out. I can't stop talking about it because it was such a joyful discovery for me! So off we went, and we spent six more weeks exploring our basic Christian doctrines. (Even if you are not United Methodist, you may have a similar guide.)

There is something to say about being radical, but there is also something to say about knowing not everything will go as you had originally planned. Don't believe me? Just ask our church trustees. All right. We told you earlier that we would explain why the board of trustees is hesitant when it comes to our use of candles. Here we go. It was during this "Basic Christian Doctrine" series that the incident occurred. We thought it would be fun to have people draw or paint or otherwise express on paper their understanding of some of the basics of our faith. We took these sheets of butcher paper and hung them around the worship space. Around the perimeter we had various tables and we were liberal with our use of candles—you know, to create the mood. One such banner referenced the Holy Spirit as the One Who Sanctifies us. Now we happened to be talking about the Holy Spirit that night when all of a sudden it happened. On the side of the room, a fire broke out. The banner—the Holy Spirit Banner—was ablaze. Several people were immediately there to put it out before any permanent damage was done.

However, we must be totally honest. On one hand, we were thankful for the quick response time of our church members. On another slightly dysfunctional hand, we were excited that the

Holy Spirit had caught fire! I don't know if we were going for the Upper Room effect, but we kind of got it. We prayed that the Lord would cause His people to catch fire with the Holy Spirit in a real and powerful way, and that we were thankful the building did not suffer any more damage. And in case you are wondering, we have convinced the trustees to continue letting us use candles, but with extreme caution.

To conclude these uplifting thoughts on failing, refer to Psalm 46:10. I have to remind myself of these words often as, sadly, we as the church spend so much time running that we forget to slow down and listen to the One who is ready to speak and lead those ready to seek Him out.

> "Be still, and know that I am God;
> I will be exalted among the nations,
> I will be exalted in the earth." (Psalm 46:10 NIV)

Post that scripture somewhere so when you think it is all about you, guess what? It's not.

CHAPTER 8

BE FEARLESS

Jesus promised his disciples three things—that they would be
completely fearless, absurdly happy and in constant trouble.
—G. K. Chesterton

A pastor once told me a story about when their church began going in a more "charismatic" direction. Some people began to raise their hands as an act of worship during the singing. People were clapping and some danced at their seats. Some even stepped out into the aisle because they needed more room to dance before the Lord. There was even a group who would gather down front and dance the dances of their Celtic homeland. Some found the passage about the Lord being our Banner and so they actually made banners and began to wave them around during the singing and dancing part of worship. It was becoming quite a lively service. In light of this, the pastor said one person came to him out of concern. This gentleman stated that he was uncomfortable with the direction of the worship services and wanted to make sure things were under control. The pastor lovingly told him not to worry, that the leadership would make sure that nothing occurred that was not found in the Bible. This concerned gentleman nodded his head in affirmation of the acceptable response. His fears were calmed and he began to leave. The pastor called after the man. "Did you hear what I said? We will not do anything that is not found in the Scriptures. Have you even read the Bible?! That ought to scare the hell out of you!"

I love this story for so many reasons. It demonstrates to me how so many people either don't know the Bible, don't know the power and the stories found in the Scriptures, or they don't know the power of the dangerously high calling of the One who transcends them. It is a serious mistake, in my opinion borderline heresy, to teach that the invitation to follow Jesus will naturally result in a safe and prosperous life. We can really send the wrong impression if we don't clarify the difference between prosperity from a biblical standpoint and that of twenty-first–century American culture. As so many others have stated before, we want to be careful that we don't measure success in terms of how big a building we can build, or how many peopple we can cram into it, or how much money we have in our bank accounts. The world does not need churches tying up money in accounts when there is so much that could be done. I am not saying we need to recklessly spend money, but we don't need to be so afraid, so captivated by fear, that we never actually use it. Erwin McManus states that the minute a church seeks to maintain itself, it is dead.[1]

For just a moment look at the following verses from Genesis, chapter 12:

> The LORD had said to Abram, "Leave your country, your people and your father's household and go to the land I will show you.

"I will make you into a great nation and I will bless you;
I will make your name great,
    and you will be a blessing.
I will bless those who bless you,
    and whoever curses you I will curse;
and all peoples on earth
    will be blessed through you." (vv. 1-3 NIV)

It is in the first couple of verses here that we gain great insight into why we as the church exist. God has had a purpose for His people from the very beginning, and that purpose has not changed, even until today. God desires to bless His people. But it is not for their own sake, and isn't this where we so many times get it wrong? God does this so we will go and be a blessing to others, and more important, that others may come into a saving relationship with the Lord Almighty. We are given much to make the name of God known. Sometimes that is risky. Many times that causes us to be uncomfortable. Oftentimes it means getting our hands, our feet, even our lives, dirty.

To be in relationship with people is a messy thing. Is it a risk to help others? Of course it is. But Jesus Christ did not invite us to follow him that we might be safe in this world. In truth he said that we would likely encounter danger and risk death. Can I ask a question? When did we turn the words of Jesus into a safe message? God called Abram to leave everything. *Everything*! There is nothing safe about that. But God promised He would be with Abram. And that is an assurance that transcends any fear in this world. Remember the story of Aslan in the *Chronicles of Narnia*? Lucy asks if Aslan is safe. " 'Course he isn't safe," Mr. Beaver replies. "But he's good." [2] What a beautiful and powerful image. The Lord of all creation is not safe. But oh, how God is good.

My brothers and sisters, may you be empowered to dream big. May you take time to listen to the voice of God, and may you be unafraid to shout from the rooftops what you hear whispered into your ear. May you hear the call of

Dream BIG.

Christ saying, "Step outside the boat," and with such wild abandon, may you not just step but leap. May you live and lead with a passion that screams the message of Jesus Christ. May you light candles, drop seashells, dance like David, and make trustees nervous for the glory of God. May you praise, may you study, may you pray, and may you commune with God, and in so doing may you discover a joy, a peace, and a confident assurance that the Lord is with you always. Be bold, be great, be grace, be love, be fearless, and in all places, just give them Jesus.

NOTES

Introduction

1. Thanks to John Piper for this phrase. John Piper is the pastor of Bethlehem Baptist Church in Minneapolis. His ministry centers on the theme, "God is most glorified in us when we are most satisfied in Him." This theme is prevalent throughout his works. More information of John Piper and his ministry and resources can be found at www.desiringgod.org.

2. H. B. London Jr. and Neil B. Wiseman, *The Heart of a Great Pastor: How to Grow Strong and Thrive Wherever God Has Planted You* (Ventura, Calif.: Regal Books, 1994), dedication.

2. Worship Worth Giving Your Life For

1. Neil Cole beautifully and powerfully explores this in his book *Organic Church: Growing Faith Where Life Happens* (San Francisco: Jossey-Bass, 2005).

2. Tom Tenny, *God Chasers* (Shippensburg, Pa.: Destiny Image, 1998), 19–20. This idea is developed extensively in chapter 2 of *God Chasers*, which is well worth reading in full.

3. Joel Kiekintveld, "Blues, Beer, and the Kingdom of God," www.theooze.com (June 2003). See http://www.theooze.com/articles/article.cfm?id=534&page=1.

4. John Leland, "Alt-worship: Christian Cool and the New Generation Gap," *New York Times* (May 16, 2004).

5. Often attributed, perhaps incorrectly, to John Wesley.

6. Rick Warren, *The Purpose Driven Life* (Philadelphia, Pa.: Miniature Editions, 2003), 100.

7. Henry Blackaby and Claude V. King, *Experiencing God*, workbook edition (Nashville: Lifeway Press, 1990), 29.

3. Reclaiming the Power of Worship through PRAISE

1. Darlene Zschech, "Extravagant Worship" (2001), www.integritymusic.com/worship/zschech/0901.html.

2. "Dance Like David" is a song written by Mark Sorensen and is available for preview at his website, www.mark-sorensen.com.

4. Reclaiming the Power of Worship through PRAYER

1. Louie Giglio has done an amazing job communicating this truth. I highly encourage you to find his message about our indescribable God; read his book *I Am Not, but I Know I AM* (Sisters, Ore.: Multnomah Publishers, 2005), and get lost in the power and awe of our marvelous God.
2. Matt Redman, "Blessed Be Your Name," *Blessed Be Your Name: The Songs of Matt Redman*, vol. 1 (Six Steps Records, 2005).
3. E. M. Bounds, *E. M. Bounds on Prayer* (New Kensington, Pa.: Whitaker House, 1997), 11.
4. See www.csm.org.

5. Reclaiming the Power of Worship through STUDY

1. See 1 Samuel 3:8-10 for more on this dangerous statement!

6. Reclaiming the Power of Worship through COMMUNION

1. See http://www.gbod.org/worship/greatthanksgiving-tucker06.pdf.

7. Be Willing to Fail

1. John Piper, *Don't Waste Your Life* (Wheaton, Ill.: Crossway Books, 2003), 45–46.
2. "Provide" lyrics, chord sheets, and a free audio preview available at www.mark-sorensen.com.
3. "Heal Me, Lord" lyrics, chord sheets, and a free audio preview available at www.mark-sorensen.com.

8. Be Fearless

1. Erwin Raphael McManus, *Unstoppable Force: Daring to Become the Church God Had in Mind* (Loveland, Colo.: Group, 2001), 22–23.
2. C. S. Lewis, *The Lion, the Witch, and the Wardrobe* (New York: Collier Books, 1970), 75–76.